100

CONTROVERSIAL

(Newspaper)

COLUMNS

-Spiritual thoughts from a layman who has struggled through the same

questions and answers you have-

WILLIE HOLT

100 CONTROVERSIAL COLUMNS

© **2015 by Willie Holt**

All rights reserved. No part of this book may be reproduced in any form or by any means, without written permission by the publisher, except by a reviewer who may quote brief passages in a review.

Published by MaxHoltMedia
303 Cascabel Place, Mount Juliet, TN 37122
www.maxholtmedia.com

The author is totally responsible for the content and the editing of this work and Max Holt Media offers no warranty, expressed or implied, or assumes any legal liability or responsibility for the accuracy and completeness of any information contained herein. The author bears responsibility for obtaining permission to use any portion of this work that may be the intellectual property of another person or organization.

Cover Design: Max Holt Media
Cover Art: ID 28887234 © Hdcphoto | Dreamtime.com
      Columns support roof of government building

ISBN 13: 978-0-9966104-7-6

INTRODUCTION

These devotional thoughts appeared in a weekly column that was written for a small newspaper. Since many people enjoyed the columns and made comments about them, I thought it might do the same for others in a wider outreach, in the form of a book. These spiritual thoughts are not written to challenge or hinder anyone's faith or personal beliefs; I am sure all people have questions about various subjects.

So, this book of *discussions* may provide thoughts others might like to discuss, or inject their own thoughts. We are living in an advanced world, and many of the old values have been ignored or discarded completely. This book may serve to recall a few of them to our minds. We may not be able to change anything, but we can be reminded of, and discuss some of the past values we once knew.

ENJOY!

Willie Holt

CONTENTS

1. BEFORE CREATION
2. THE FALL
3. HOW OLD IS GOD'S CREATION?
4. LET OUR LIGHT SHINE
5. GOD'S POWER
6. LISTEN TO THE BOSS (GOD)
7. THE RICHES OF THE WORLD
8. ALL CREATION BELONGS TO GOD THE SON
9. DOES GOD EXIST?
10. CHRISTIAN SERVICE TO OTHERS
11. INTENTIONALLY SERVING GOD
12. WHERE IS YOUR TREASURE?
13. WHAT GOD HATES
14. RIGHTEOUSNESS
15. CHANGES
16. TRIALS
17. THOUGHTS ABOUT JOB'S TROUBLES
18. GIVING GLORY TO GOD
19. HIDING OUR SINS
20. SET YOURSELF FREE
21. DOES GOD EXIST?
22. THE GREATEST BATTLE GROUND
23. GETTING ATTENTION
24. DOUBTING GOD
25. AMERICA'S CONSTITUTION
26. REPENTING OF OUR SINS
27. CHRISTIANS' POWER
28. MOVING GOD OUT
29. CATASTROPHES
30. GOD'S TEMPLE TODAY
31. HUM-DRUM
32. A MADE UP STORY
33. TAKING CARE OF OUR BODIES
34. TIME
35. OUR FREE CHOICE
36. THANKFUL
37. SLOW DETERIORATION
38. GOSSIP
39. THE DEATH, BURIAL, AND RESURRECTION OF JESUS CHRIST

40. GOD-GIVEN TALENTS
41. DISARMING THE PUBLIC
42. TRUST
43. THE LIES WE TELL
44. OUR SPOKEN WORDS
45. THE HOLY SPIRIT
46. PRAYER WITHOUT WORDS
47. PROCRASTINATION
48. PUSH, PUSH, PUSH
49. THE SECOND COMING
50. ONE ROAD TO HEAVEN
51. THE HOLY BIBLE, THE BEST BOOK
52. OBEY THE RULES
53. SIGNS OF THE TIMES
54. MANY GODS
55. NO DEFENSE
56. GOD BECAME A MAN
57. OUR FINAL DECISION
58. THE SEE-SAW OF LIFE
59. GOD'S DECREE
60. SPIRITUAL HAZE
61. THE CHURCH'S DECLINE
62. HONORING GOD
63. MY PLAN VERSUS GOD'S PLAN
64. REAL FAITH
65. RECEIVING RIGHTEOUSNESS
66. SODOM AND GOMORRAH
67. TEST ON PLANT LIFE
68. CHRISTIAN JOY
69. AT YOUR HOUSE
70. WHAT YOU DO
71. TWO DOGS INSIDE
72. ROAD MAP TO HEAVEN
73. THE BODY AND SOUL
74. THE SUBSTANCE OF HOPE
75. GOD CAME
76. THE SEVENTH CHURCH
77. CHRISTIAN DUTY
78. DOING THINGS MY WAY
79. GOOD VERSUS EVIL
80. KNOWLEDGE
81. CHRISTIAN UNDERSTANDING
82. MY OLD SELF AND MY NEW SELF

83. ABOUT KING SOLOMON
84. OUR RELATIONSHIP WITH GOD
85. THE HEART CHRISTIAN
    VERSUS THE MIND CHRISTIAN
86. THE TREE OF LIFE AND THE
    TREE OF DEATH
87. CHRISTIAN WORKS
88. TRUE BELIEF
89. RIGHTEOUS ENOUGH
90. WHO DOES GOD CALL?
91. SOME EXPLANATION
92. DOER'S OF THE WORD
93. STRANGE THINGS ARE HAPPENING
94. PILLS, PILLS
95. A DISCUSSION
96. GOD WITH US
97. THE CORD OF SIN
98. TEMPTED TO SIN
99. BE A MAN
100. THE LAW FULFILLED

"We have been assured, Sir, in the Sacred Writings, that 'except the LORD build the House, they labor in vain that build it.' I firmly believe this; by our partial local interests our projects will be confounded and we ourselves shall become a reproach and a by-word down to future ages"

Benjamin Franklin

1 - BEFORE CREATION

Before GOD made the plan for creation, He created three mighty angels, one for each of His three persons; one (Michael) for GOD the Father, one (Lucifer) for GOD the Son, and one (Gabriel) for the GOD the Holy Spirit.

Each Mighty Angel was given a host of other angels to serve under them. Michael was given the power to carry out the will of GOD the Father tending His affairs. Lucifer was given great beauty and the power to lead the Heavenly Choir. Gabriel was given the power to deliver GOD's messages wherever He was sent. Lucifer, (the angel of GOD the Son) saw his beauty one time and decided he should move his throne up to the level of GOD the Father's throne.

Since GOD hated the pride and sin found in Lucifer and would not share His Glory with anyone or anything, Lucifer was cast down and his host of angels with him. Lucifer's name was changed to Satan because he originated sin and caused all his angels to fall with him. Satan went into a great rage and vowed to destroy everything GOD did from then on.

The plan for creation was then made, maybe to replace Lucifer and his angels; we do not know for sure. All we know is, the Bible says all things were created for GOD the Son, Jesus Christ. All things were made for Him and by Him. Remember, Lucifer was created for GOD the Son and was not satisfied with his place and was cast out.

PAUSE FOR EXPLANATION: Actually, GOD being three persons, yet one, is not a great mystery. Humans are three persons, yet one. One can hold a job, be a husband, and a father all at the same time; three different persons, yet one. The great mystery is that we cannot be at work, be with our wives, and play with the kids all at the same time; but GOD can. That is the great mystery. GOD can be everywhere at the same time and still be one GOD.

GOD finalized His plan for creation and began work on the first day. It was one day because *morning and evening* refer to one rotation of the Earth. GOD completed His creation in six days and rested on the seventh day. He created grass for the animals, seeds for the birds, and fruit for humans. He created a layer of oxygen around for all to breathe and trees to keep the oxygen replenished.

When GOD looked at all He had done, He said that it was good, and surely very beautiful. He created Adam in His own image and breathed into his nostrils so Adam became a living soul. Adam could think, make decisions, and walk and talk with GOD. GOD placed every kind of fruit tree in the Garden of Eden as food for Adam and Eve and told Adam to till the ground and keep it clean and watered.

BOTTOM LINE: GOD's initial plan was *ALL GOOD*. But, mankind couldn't leave *perfection* alone. You will see in the following 99 devotionals what we have done to it.

Your Notes & Scriptures:

2 – THE FALL

We talk about wars and rumors of wars, but what about the spiritual war going on all around us which we cannot see with our natural eyes? We have the account of the fall of Adam and Eve in the Garden of Eden. I think we need to understand all that happened on that day.

When GOD created Adam, He breathed the breath of life into Adam's nostrils and Adam became a living soul. That means GOD imparted a part of himself into Adam, which would cause Adam to desire to walk and talk with GOD and have fellowship with Him. When Adam and Eve sinned against GOD, Satan entered into Adam's flesh; mind. The war fought for the souls of mankind is between GOD and Satan and is fought in our minds. Whichever one controls our minds controls us. GOD said in His Word, *"the spirit is willing but the flesh is weak."* Since Satan has put his nature into our flesh, we want to have everything the world has to offer; good times, ease of life, a happy lifestyle, riches, honor, and all the attention we can get from others.

GOD's love for mankind has not changed since the day He created Adam in His own image. GOD wants every human to come to him and enjoy eternal life, however, GOD knew from the beginning that Adam and Eve would not be able to resist the Devil's temptation to rebel against GOD and eat from the Tree of Knowledge, of Good and Evil, so they would be like GOD Himself. GOD knew all this at the time He was making the plan for creation. Some people believe GOD asked the question: *"Who will go and pay the price for sin and buy back the souls of mankind?"*

They also believe that GOD the Son then said: *"Since the angel that fell was mine and has caused the fall of mankind, I will go to Earth and become a man so I can die and pay the sin debt for all people."* Only GOD Himself could do that!

The plan was finalized and everything happened just as GOD foresaw in His great foreknowledge. Today, we are in the same battle Adam was in when he was tempted in the Garden. Temptations are everywhere and constantly with us. The good part is that GOD will not allow Satan to tempt us more than we can stand. In the Bible book of Job, GOD always told Satan just how far he could go to bring disaster on Job.

BOTTOM LINE: Satan is *always* under GOD's control, even when he is testing and tempting us.

Your Notes & Scriptures:

3 - HOW OLD IS GOD'S CREATION?

We were not there when GOD created the heavens and the Earth. However, we have a few clues found in the Bible.

First: In the Bible, in the New Testament book of Luke, the generations from Adam to the first coming of Jesus Christ are listed and total to about 4000 years, and the time from Jesus Christ to the present is about 2000 years making a total of 6000+ years.

Second: According to Dr. Kent Hovind the carbon dating is based on the amount of carbon being formed outside the atmosphere versus the amount falling to the Earth. The balance of the same amount falling to the amount being formed has been determined to be 25,000 years, however when the measurements were made, it was found the process has only been going on between 6000 and 7000 years. Some said a mistake was made in the measurements; however no one has ever found it.

Third: Adam and Eve were created without sin. Sin did not exist. That means death did not exist either because death came because of sin. Since death did not exist before sin and sin came on the Earth about 6000+ years ago, no living being could have lived and died before that time.

Fourth: When GOD started His creation, He marked the days by saying, *"...the morning and the evening were the first day."* That was one rotation of the Earth; 24 hours. So GOD really did create the heavens and the Earth in six days. No wonder He rested on the seventh day!

Another point: GOD told Adam he could eat from any tree in the Garden of Eden except the Tree of Knowledge of Good and Evil and the day he ate from that tree, he would die. We know Adam did not die physically when he ate the forbidden fruit, but he did die spiritually that day and died physically in less than one thousand years, one of GOD's *days*. So GOD's Word stands.

BOTTOM LINE: There is no use kidding ourselves; GOD is not keeping anything from us, but has given us all the knowledge we are able to absorb. I believe GOD invites us to find out all we can about Him and His Heavenly home, His creation, and our Earthly home by studying His Word. The more we find out about GOD, the more we can trust Him and His Word to be perfect and true. Not being a wise old GURU, I cannot stand on a street corner and proclaim all of this as absolute truth, but if I can cause someone to start thinking about it, my purpose is served.

P. S. Don't blame GOD is you are not blessed.

Your Notes & Scriptures:

4 – LET OUR LIGHT SHINE

As Christians, we are commanded to let our light shine so the *lost* world can see GOD in us and desire to come to GOD for forgiveness of sin and the gift of eternal salvation.

First: Our light must be bright enough for the world to see.

Second: Our light comes only from GOD, the Father of lights.

Third: The light shines brightest when we are in GOD's will.

Fourth: The world only sees our face, so that is where our light must shine. If we are full of sin and worldly desires, our light will be so dim no one can see it.

We may say we are Christians, but if it can't be seen, we will not influence anyone. We are not talking about a silly grin, but a look of faith in the GOD we serve, the joy He brings to His children, and the peace of mind GOD gives to us when we trust Him. Joy will come when we serve others. Brighten someone's day be giving them a big smile, call someone and tell them the latest *clean* joke you have heard, take a few of your cookies to the neighbor next door, invite someone to join you in a Bible study in your home, or just chat with the neighbors across the fence.

Preachers and pastors are just as human as anyone else. They love to be told they are doing a good job preaching or teaching the Word. It is always good to tell the preacher you stayed awake and heard his message, and hope he don't ask you what the message was about.

Being human, we very often act and think like the people we fellowship with. Jesus knew this when He told His disciples to love one another and have fellowship with one another. He knew Christians would draw more strength from each other than anyone else.

The Devil hates the light we get from GOD and does everything in his power to make it dim and useless as a witness for GOD and His kingdom. The Devil has slowly brought things into our homes through the television, computers, cell phones, and any other source he can find, which we should not see or hear. If the Devil can control our minds, he wins the battle and makes us no use to GOD or the Church

BOTTOM LINE: Walking with GOD every day is not easy, but there is great joy in just being close to Him. I believe GOD will bend very low toward the Earth to hear the slightest whisper from one of His children and will make Himself known to them in every situation.

Your Notes & Scriptures:

5 – GOD'S POWER

We talk about wars and rumors of wars, but what about the spiritual war going on all around us, which we cannot see with our natural eyes? We have the account of the fall of Adam and eve in the Garden of Eden. I think we need to understand all that happened on that day.

When GOD created Adam, He breathed the breath of life into Adam's nostrils and Adam became a living soul. That means GOD imparted a part of himself into Adam which would cause Adam to desire to walk and talk with GOD and have fellowship with Him. When the Devil was able to cause Adam and Eve to disobey GOD and sin against Him, Satan then imparted a part of himself into Adam and Eve, namely all things opposing GOD and His commandments. GOD's part was placed in Adam's soul, *the spiritual part of Adam* and was pure and holy. Satan's part was placed in Adams body, *the flesh,* and was evil and rebellious against GOD and all good.

The war fought for the souls of mankind is between GOD and Satan and is fought in our minds. Whichever one controls our minds controls us. GOD said in His Word, *"the spirit is willing but the flesh is weak"*. Since Satan has put his nature into our flesh, we want to have everything the world has to offer, good times, ease of life, a happy lifestyle, riches, honor, and all the attention we can get from others.

GOD's love for mankind has not changed since the day He created Adam in His own image. GOD wants every human to come to Him and enjoy eternal life, however, GOD knew from the beginning that Adam and Eve would not be able to resist the Devil's temptation to rebel against GOD and eat from the Tree of Knowledge of Good and Evil, so they would be like GOD Himself. GOD knew all this at the time He was making the plan of creation. Some people believe GOD asked the question, *"Who will go and pay the price for sin and buy back the souls of mankind?"* GOD the Son then said, *"Since the Angel that fell was mine and has caused the fall of mankind, I will go to Earth and become a man so I can die and pay the sin debt for all people."* Only GOD Himself could do that!

The plan was finalized and everything happened just as GOD foresaw in His great foreknowledge. Today, we are in the same battle Adam was in when they was tempted in the Garden. Temptations are everywhere and constantly with us. The good part is, GOD will not allow Satan to tempt us more than we can stand. In the Bible book of Job, GOD always told Satan just how far he could go, bringing disaster on Job.

BOTTOM LINE: As I mentioned earlier, Satan is *always* under GOD's control when he is tempting us.

Your Notes & Scriptures:

6 – LISTEN TO THE BOSS (GOD)

Once there was a man who worked for a large company. This man worked hard and was dedicated to the company. He was interested in helping the company to grow and expand. He liked his boss and was willing to listen to the boss' wisdom pertaining to company business. The boss observed this man day after day and decided he was well qualified to run the company. One day the boss decided to take an extended vacation to rest and make some important business contacts. The boss called the man into his office and explained his plan, telling him he wanted him to run the company while he was gone.

As the man settled in to his boss' office, he started to annualize and determine what had to be done to run the company efficiently and make a profit while the boss was gone. He had many ideas of his own, but something didn't quite feel right. He decided to remember and apply all of his boss' training and wisdom he had heard. Also the boss left notes and plans written down in his office and the man decided that was the best plan. The man followed his instincts and sure enough, the company grew and flourished even more than he had expected.

Another man also worked for the same company. This man was also loyal to the company and worked to advance the company. He liked his boss and was willing to listen to what the boss said. Upon leaving, the boss appointed this man a job supervising a section of the company and the man was thrilled and was determined to do good for the boss and the company. He also applied the boss' method of running this section and the section also flourished and was a better asset to the company.

A third man worked for the company and was not completely satisfied with his job and thought he had much better ideas on how the company should operate. The boss also called this man in and gave him a job supervising a smaller section of the company. Immediately, this man thought, this is my chance to show them how things should be done around here. He started applying his ideas and thoughts in buying materials and showing everybody under him how he wanted things done. Soon, some of the workers became angry and upset because this man was shouting and barking out orders continually. The section began to fail and production nearly stopped. His section was costing the company money, not making money.

BOTTOM: LINE. This story illustrates what happens when people do not listen to the boss, GOD, and follow His instructions either through the urging of the Holy Spirit, or through His notes and outlines; the Bible.

Your Notes & Scriptures:

7 – THE RICHES OF THE WORLD

What are the true riches of this world? There is money, there are large land holdings, there are large companies, there are all kinds of stuff that everybody seems to want, and of course there is the lottery, worth millions of dollars. There are super cars, yachts, mansions and vacation homes in tropical places. So, does any or all of it make one happy? Suppose a person becomes super rich and has no one to share it with. Suppose a person should spend their whole life building an empire worth a great fortune and destroy their health doing it. Can they be happy with all that? Please understand, there is nothing wrong with having any of those things, but in the end, if the person does not have at least some of the *real* precious things, it will not be worth it at all.

What are those *real* precious things in question? First of all, the *real* precious things have to be given to us. We cannot find and go and get them by ourselves. The first and most precious one is true love. The Bible says that GOD is love and He is surely the source of all love, even the love between humans here on Earth. The greatest kind of life is the kind that only GOD has for all mankind, and He wants to give us the ability to love Him with that same kind of love. The name for it is AGAPE; it is the highest and most unconditional love in existence. When a person accepts Jesus Christ as their personal Savior, GOD will give that person the power to love Him with the same kind of love. GOD will also train that person to love their friends and neighbors, and especially fellow Christians with the same love.

Another kind of love is the kind that exists between humans. It is called EROS. That is the kind of love that husbands and wives have for each other. It is the kind that a Father would have for his children, and a mother would have for her children. It can also exist between brothers and sisters and between good friends. This type of love is given to mankind by GOD so the human race can live together and work together, and have peace among themselves. The EROS love is meant to be between people. It is not acceptable to GOD for His children to offer the EROS kind of love to Him. Only the AGAPE love will be accepted by GOD. That is found in the First and Greatest Commandant; "LOVE THE LORD YOUR GOD WITH ALL YOUR HEART, ALL YOUR SOUL, BODY AND STRENGTH." That is the AGAPE love. Nothing else will do between us and GOD.

BOTTOM LINE: There are many other precious things that GOD has given to his Children; the Bible, the Holy Spirit as our teacher, the Church building for a meeting place to worship Him and have fellowship with each other, just to name a few.

Your Notes & Scriptures:

8 – ALL CREATION BELONGS TO GOD THE SON

Jesus Christ made the statement that GOD the Father had given *all things* into His hands. What that means is that Jesus owns Jupiter, Mars, Venus, and all planets and stars beyond those planets. It also means He owns the Earth and all things on this planet, including land, animals, fish and all humans. Now since that is a fact, why don't we believe it and respond accordingly? I am talking about Christians and our service to Jesus and the Church.

I believe one reason our service is diluted is that the worldly things have been increasing through television, news media and technical devices. Since we are forced to use some of those devices daily, the temptation to misuse some of them is overwhelming. We seem to need, *or want* many things of the world to make our lives better.

Although there is nothing wrong with having most things we use and enjoy, it is so easy to allow them to get in the way of our dedication and service to GOD. The Bible refers to that as neglecting our *first love*. I believe that GOD does in fact approve most of the things we use and enjoy in our daily living, but He does not want them to come between us and Him. True devotion is the one and only thing we can actually give to our GOD to show our love for Him and the fact that He took our place in death on the cross. All other abilities for service to GOD in any way must be given to us by the Holy Spirit, the gift given at the point of Salvation.

GOD has given us access to His power to be of use while He leaves us on this Earth. GOD will not allow us to use His power for our personal satisfaction. GOD's power has *not* actually been given into our hands to use at will. GOD knows that if I should get mad at someone, I would probably do a lot of harm to them if I processed any power above my own human strength.

What can we do as common people to serve GOD in a way that He will be pleased with? I believe prayer is the number one thing we can do that will please and cause GOD to be with us daily. Although prayer is surely pleasing to GOD, it is the one thing that keeps us close to GOD and living a clean life within ourselves. The Bible says that the *"prayer of a righteous man avails much,"* that is; it is a powerful force against the Devil and his devices.

BOTTOM LINE: Some people say the Devil trembles when we read the Bible, but he panics when we sincerely pray to GOD. Amen!

Your Notes & Scriptures:

9 – DOES GOD EXIST?

Can Christians prove that GOD exists and lives in Heaven? Can we prove that the Holy Spirit lives inside of us? NO, GOD is a spirit! A spirit cannot be physically seen, heard, felt, touched, or tasted. How then can we prove that He exists? Actually, unless we can detect something or someone with our five human senses, we cannot humanly prove it. In reality we cannot prove the existence of love. Of course we can show love by doing things for the one we love, but a good actor can do the same thing and make us believe it. So that leaves us with no proof. Frankly, we can prove very little in our existence, in our human bodies.

Well, suppose we could prove GOD exists, and all His angels, and Heaven. That would wipe out all need for faith. (Jesus placed a high value on faith while He was on Earth). People would treat GOD just like little kids treat their parents, by getting into trouble (sin) all day every day. And worst of all, people would try to bring GOD down to our level and bargain with Him constantly. Furthermore GOD's glory would be diluted and dragged through this sinful world.

Although we cannot even imagine the glory of GOD we believe that it is so powerful and so precious to GOD, that no one else can share it with GOD. He alone is worthy to receive the highest devotion from all of His creation. Some of us believe that GOD's glory is so bright and powerful that when GOD the Son, Jesus Christ, appears with His saints, His brightness will be the thing that causes the flesh of people to melt off their bones. And that's when the blood will run up to the bridle bits of a horse for 200 miles. I think that His appearing is the only time recorded in the Bible where that much blood could suddenly be dumped on the ground.

I cannot believe that GOD will allow anyone to rise above his existence; that is, the knowledge we are able to gain and retain is here on this Earth. GOD has given us a complete record of Himself in the Bible. I have been told that the Bible is so written that a young child can understand enough of it to accept Jesus Christ as their personal Savior, and the highest learned professor cannot exhaust the knowledge contained in it. I don't know any person who could write a book like that. Do you?

BOTTOM LINE: Sometimes I wonder just who we think we are. We built a spaceship and sent some men to the Moon but all they brought back was a sack full of rocks.

Your Notes & Scriptures:

10 – CHRISTIAN SERVICE TO OTHERS

Personal Service to others; what is it? What is it worth? Where do we start? First and most important is serving GOD. People who are *not* Christians can still serve GOD by respecting Christians and their Church. Second, Christians serve GOD by obeying His commandments, the first of which is to love GOD with all our soul, mind, and strength, and Jesus added later, "The second is to love our neighbors as ourselves." When those two commandments are obeyed, all the others fall into place with little effort. Service to the church may be to find a need and fill it. That may be to visit someone in the hospital, or visit someone confined to their home, or take some food to someone recovering from surgery, and the list goes on and on. It is always good to brighten a person's day. Call someone and tell them a joke, or just talk, or let them talk.

All buildings require maintenance, the church buildings included. If you have a certain talent of electrical, or plumbing, or general construction, you will often find a place to use your talents for the church. Just remember, mankind was not created to be idle, or to sit back with an open mouth for GOD to fill all day. We should remember that Adam and Eve were made to till the Garden of Eden and take care of it. It feels *so good* to serve GOD in some way with the right attitude and purpose. It seems that GOD always loves for His children to do that. You can be sure of this; that kind of service it will not go unnoticed.

Service to the community involves caring about trash lying around, caring about and supporting our City Government, caring about the safety of our children, caring about the residents of our city and their wellbeing. Volunteer work is always needed in several areas. You can bet that the opportunities for service are always endless.

I believe serving in our own homes is just as important as serving anywhere else. If GOD entrusted to us a home, cars, money in the bank, and a family, then we surely are expected to take care of them. That must mean taking care of the yard, keeping the house repaired, taking care of the cars, being responsible for our money in the bank, and most of all taking care of our family. That would involve sharing responsible with the wife for watching over and training the children, and inner workings of the house. NOTE: All of these things will work well if we will keep GOD in the *center* of our comings and goings.

BOTTOM LINE: Let us do it.

Your Notes & Scriptures:

11 – INTENTIONALLY SERVING GOD

If our service to GOD and fellow humans is going to be worth anything, it must be intentional. In fact, everything we do should be intentional; our jobs, our families, our church, and neighbors. If we don't get interested in what we are doing, it will not be worth anything.

On our jobs, we usually work for a company, and that company must make a profit on our labor to stay in business. To be valuable to the company, we must do the job the best we can, and help promote the company's business.

Likewise, if we are going to take care of our families in a way that will be pleasing to GOD, it must be intentional. That is, the care should be based on the Bible teaching about family care; the man's roll, the woman's roll, and the children's roll. HINT: *A day hemmed in prayer is not easily unraveled, especially Morning Prayers.*

Our church building is a place set aside to meet to worship GOD and fellowship with one another. It could be referred to as a Filling Station, because that is where we go to get recommitted to GOD's Holy Spirit so we can make it to the next time we meet. I am sure we all know the problems and trials we face daily take a toll on our own Spirit. A renewal is refreshing and necessary to remain true in service to GOD through the church.

Serving GOD by serving our neighbors is another important part of our stay on this Earth. I find that I can truly love my neighbors as myself as long as they behave and don't cause me any trouble. However, they don't always do that. That is when I need GOD's Spirit to help me act right in my neighborhood. Sometimes, just a wave cross the street causes a smile. Sometimes, baking a few extra cookies and taking some to a neighbor works well, or inviting someone over for a meal is good. If we always remember to do all this in the name of the Lord Jesus Christ, and show a Christian attitude, that is a powerful witness for the Lord.

We live in a world that is filled with all kinds of corruption and self serving people. Living a sin-free life in this world may be like walking through a jungle without touching any of the leaves of the trees; it is just impossible. I believe that is one reason GOD has granted forgiveness for all our sins for the rest of our lives. With a commitment like that, it becomes easier to love the Lord with all our heart, and soul, and mind. If GOD had not made a commitment like that, we would not have a chance to escape the eternal punishment the *lost* will go into.

BOTTOM LINE: Maybe *NOW* would be the right time call on God and renew our Christian Commitment.

Your Notes & Scriptures:

12 – WHERE IS YOUR TREASURE?

Where is your treasure? Is it in the bank? Is it in your possessions? Is it in your family? Is it in your church? Is it in your country? Is it in your job?---OR---Is it in HEAVEN?

One bad Illness can wipe out your bank account. One bad fire or accident can wipe out your possessions. One bad split can wipe out your church. A bad economy can almost wipe out your country. One bad bodily accident can wipe out your job. But, none of those things or anyone here or there can even come near your treasure in Heaven. Neither thieves, or bad behavior, or sin, not the Devil's threat can take away one kind word spoken to someone who needs it. GOD has promised to personally guard our treasure in Heaven. I believe that if our treasure in Heaven is that important to GOD, it should be very precious to us. GOD has encouraged us to *"LAY UP treasures in Heaven,"* instead of on this Earth. I think that should make it clear what our goal in this life should be.

This plan to lay up treasures in Heaven is meant for true Christians only. A true Christian is a person who has been born again. That means the true Christian has discovered they are a sinner and cannot reach Heaven by their own deeds, no matter how good they are. GOD's demand for perfect righteousness far exceeds our ability to achieve it. The only person on Earth who ever met GOD's requirement of a sinless life was Jesus Christ Himself. When He paid our sin debt by giving His life on the cross, He made it possible for us to obtain *His* righteousness by faith and cause GOD to forgive our sins and make us acceptable in His sight.

When a person is *born again*, the past sins in their soul are removed and cast away out of GOD's sight, never to be brought up again. However since GOD knows the future, and that we cannot always resist temptation, He extended His forgiveness for the rest of our lives. Although we will be taken to the *wood shed* now and then by GOD Himself, He will not withdraw his promise to take us to Heaven when this life is over. It can't get any better than that! Who can blame people for having a hard time believing that, *because we are natural sinners*, but it is true. You can read the Bible from front to back, and you will never find where GOD threw out one of His own children. GOD is nothing like us, and never will be.

BOTTOM LINE: The choice has been given to us to decide if we are willing to accept GOD's plan or not. I hope you are not one of those *NOT* people.

Your Notes & Scriptures:

13 – WHAT GOD HATES

The seven abominations that GOD hates: #1 A proud look.......#2 A lying tongue.......#3 Hands that shed innocent blood.......#4 A heart that devises wicked imaginations.....#5 Feet that are swift in running to mischief.......#6 A false witness that speaks lies......#7 He that sows discord among the brethren.

It seems common for us to say, *"Well I don't do any of those things"*. So maybe we should look at them one at a time.

#1 - There are times when we should take pride in ourselves, such as keeping clean personally. We should try to wear clean clothes. We should keep our houses clean, and other times, behave properly before GOD and man. But when we allow our pride to cause us to brag about our good deeds and all those times when we rise up and do something good, then it becomes sin and that is the number one item on GOD's list of things He hates. It is GOD who gives us the knowledge and strength to do anything. I believe He hates it when we try to take the credit for the talents He has given us.

#2 - We actually started telling lies before we could walk. We gave Mama those *big eyes innocent look*. Soon after that, we did that *"not me, not me"* routine and from there it got worse until we didn't notice it anymore. We have those thoughts that telling the truth would hurt someone and we sure don't want to do that.

#3 - It seems that people are being killed for the least causes today. Some are killed because they are in the way during a robbery. Others are killed because they make someone mad. I heard a story where two men killed each other on the highway when they fired their guns at the same time. Road rage is present on almost every highway. Tempers are short. Things haven't changed much since men were dueling several centuries ago. None of us are immune to these things, so you can see why we need GOD more than ever today. GOD is the only one who can make an end to the violence all around us, and He will when He gets ready.

#4 - How often do we quickly make a plan for revenge on a person who does something to us? Someone runs in front of us on the highway, or lies about us, or just doesn't do right. That's our human side. Resisting those temptations is never easy; in fact we cannot without GOD's help.

#5 - As humans we love mischief. When our little kids do something cute and a little naughty we laugh and are often proud of them. We often do a little mischief ourselves when we pull a joke on someone. I'm sure there are several different levels of mischief, but most of us are not smart enough to know the difference. Maybe we should just stay away from all of it.

#6 - It is so strange that we can have a friend for many years but if someone tells us a story about them, we tend to believe it more often than not. Sometimes our old human nature is a monster we have to face and ask for GOD's help to overcome it. It seems this old nature we have inherited searches for scandal more than truth. We love the *juicy* gossip more than the dull stuff (truth).

#7 - How often have we seen churches split because the members could not agree on something? How often have we seen *busy bodies* spreading rumors and tales in the church? It seems that once a rumor has been spread, it is nearly impossible to recall it and make things right. Some people actually have fun doing things like that.

By looking at the seven things that GOD hates, we can see our dilemma in trying to live a life pleasing to GOD. I believe the problems like this that we face, are the main reason GOD had to give us forgiveness for life. GOD gives us the power to resist evil. If we use His power to resist temptations, the power He gave us will grow stronger, but if we resist GOD's power and give in to temptation, then the power will grow weaker. We have no strength within ourselves to resist evil. If we are not willing to use GOD's power, then we will fail every time.

BOTTOM LINE: We should remember we all live in this world where all the evil things exist. Just because we are Christians does not exempt us from troubles. The greatest thing though that we have is GOD'S promise of help in time of need, and eternal life when this one is over. Praise the Lord! GOD's love and grace is all that stands between us and eternity in a lake of *real* fire, or an eternity with Him in a place of unspeakable beauty and peace. Make no mistake, GOD is not mocked, He knows each thought we have in this life. He is willing to grant us forgiveness if we will ask and accept it.

Your Notes & Scriptures:

The key to success is…to keep growing in all areas of life - mental, emotional, spiritual, as well as physical.

Julius Erving

14 – RIGHTEOUSNESS

RIGHTEOUSNESS: Where does it come from? How do we get it, so we can enter into GOD's presence?

When GOD made the plan of salvation, He knew that only He could supply the righteousness necessary to stand in His presence, so the plan was made before the world was made. The plan includes, cleaning the person's soul of all past sins (when they accept Jesus as their personal Savior). Then the Holy Spirit moves into that person's soul and puts a seal around it. When that happens, GOD begins to teach that person His commandments and instructions from the Bible. GOD's teaching also includes how to live daily for Him, and face trials and temptations which come upon us daily. GOD wants us to know that He is always standing by to see that our trials are not too much for us to overcome. We overcome trials by faith in GOD's presence and His watch care over us.

We have no righteousness in our bodies (*our flesh*) to come before GOD. The prayers we pray are presented to GOD by the Holy Spirit. When we make our requests *(prayers),* the Holy Spirit presents them to GOD and He makes the final decision. One thing we can be sure of is that the answer we get from GOD is always for our best interest. Sometimes we don't like the answer we get but we can know that GOD's answer is the very best.

What advantage is it to live in GOD's will? When Christians try to live in GOD's will, they will find love, joy, peace, and a great crowd of fellow Christians to have fellowship with. Although trials do come, GOD is right there to help in time of need. Also, GOD gives Christians forgiveness for life. We know we sin daily, *(GOD knows too)*, but we know we have a perfect *Lawyer* standing up for us before GOD day and night. His name is Jesus Christ. I personally believe the name Jesus is His Earthly name and Christ is His heavenly name. So, in Jesus Christ we can reach all the way into Heaven.

Many people who claim to be Christians are not really *born again* Christians. Some may think they are, but have never really accepted Jesus Christ and His *free* gift of Salvation. It seems that many are trying to *work* their way into Heaven. Although they may work hard their whole lives, it is all in vain. The Bible is very clear that *all* our righteousness is like filthy rags in GOD's sight. Salvation is GOD's gift to us who by faith will accept it as such. The only way into GOD's presence is by faith in Jesus and His death, burial, and resurrection. That means when GOD sees the righteousness of His Son Jesus Christ in us, we are always in His favor.

BOTTOM LIME: Let's do things GOD's way.

Your Notes & Scriptures:

15 – CHANGES

CHANGES: How much change do we need? We hear so much about change these days. My question is, change from what, to what? Would we be better off with a different Government? It seems we have gone so far down that now there is no remedy. Where will it end and what will our lifestyle be like under the change? It seems to me that our resources are being depleted daily and it does not seem like we can do much about it.

There is a place where no change has ever been, nor will ever be. That is GOD and His Kingdom. By His great love for mankind, He has extended an invitation to all people to come live with Him after this world has run its course and is destroyed. For those people who are tired of the troubles of this world and are hoping for a better one, GOD says, *"By faith in my Son Jesus Christ, I will forgive all your sins and bring you in to live with me in my perfect paradise."* I don't see how an invitation could be any better than that.

It seems that the forces of evil are working harder than ever today in many different ways. We are having sinful stuff come into our homes through the TV, Radio, and Computer. Some things have been brought in so slowly that we are accustomed to them, and it does not bother us. I think even the most unlearned Christian can see that the Devil and his hosts are working 24/7 to dilute the Christian faith and witness before the world. This business about trying to throw GOD and His Word out of America is one example of the decay of what the Christian values once stood for. I think the men who wrote our

Constitution, Laws, and Bill Of Rights understood what is needed to have freedom.

GOD has not changed His mind about giving freedom to all people. The real reason we are in such a mess is; men started trying to take GOD's place and improve on GOD's system. I remember reading about a *Mighty Angel* who tried to do that before the world was created. As I recall the reading, the *Mighty Angel* was thrown out of GOD's presence and is now waiting for certain destruction when the New Heaven and Earth are made.

As we can see with our own eyes, many events that are happening in our world are written in the Bible's book, The Revelation. I believe Jesus told His disciples that when they saw these things happening, to look up because the time would be close when He would call His Saints up to meet Him in the air.

BOTTOM LINE: I believe the names Jesus calls will be those written in His Book. Maybe we should think about these things a little more.

Your Notes & Scriptures:

16 – TRIALS

Surrendering ourselves, *our will*, to GOD is one of the hardest things for us to do sometimes. The old *nature* is often a *monster* we have to fight whenever it raises its ugly head. It seems that since we have come so far in this life, and seen so many changes, we sometimes think we have a better plan than GOD. If GOD should tell me to start on a certain row and gather the grapes, I would say, *"That row over there is better because it has more grapes."* So, we seem to try GOD's patience daily. Some folks think that we are splashing around in the toilet, *personally and nationwide*, and GOD might be about ready to flush it.

It is real easy to obey GOD while we are in church. It is those days during the week that we struggle with it, when we are alone and have no one to answer to. If we could see GOD and know He is there all the time, it would be easy to obey because of fear. But GOD wants us to trust Him and obey Him because we love Him and believe He really does know better than us which direction our lives should go. I sometimes wonder what our lives would be like if we would just give Him control completely.

Trusting in GOD's Word is another place where we seem to fall short. People everywhere, *including Christians,* struggle with keeping GOD's commandments written in His Word. Since most of the writings interfere with our lifestyle, we seem to find it easy to lay it, *the Bible*, aside until we have a convenient time to read it. More often than not, our *convenient* time never comes. The Bible is always under attack by people who do not want to obey its teachings. Some say it has errors in it. Others say it is outdated. The list goes on and on.

Another trial Christians face is entering into the *fun* the world is having. Our homes are flooded with the world's *fun* coming in through the TV, Radio, Computer, and other sources. Even the commercials are loaded with suggestive words and scenes. If we can think back, this kind of material has been brought in slowly until we didn't pay much attention to it.

Solomon, King of Israel, enjoyed everything a human can do. He had tons of gold and silver. He had three hundred wives, seven hundred live-in girlfriends. He had forty thousand servants in his house, and he did anything he wanted to. But when He stood back and looked at all of his life, he said, *"...vanity of vanities, all is vanity, I have not accomplished anything."* He went on to say, *"I will die just like the poor man, I cannot take one thing with me into death."* So you see, all we do here for ourselves will pass away.

BOTTOM LINE: Trust and obey GOD.

Your Notes & Scriptures:

17 – THOUGHTS ABOUT JOB'S TROUBLES

The following statements are one person's opinion and are not influenced by any other source.

Why did GOD allow Satan to attack Job, His faithful servant? Let's see if we can figure it out. Job was one of the world's most righteous men. He had seven sons and daughters. His sons and daughters were having fun parties at their homes, and Job was afraid they may not be pleasing GOD with their fun-filled living. Job offered brunt offering daily for them. Job may have thought that as long as he offered burnt offerings for them, GOD would not do anything to them.

This is one of the things that we all seem to think sometimes that as long as we go to church and be good, GOD will not do anything to us. I think that is one of the worst things we can assume. GOD is not bound by our thoughts or actions. If GOD should give me the power to move mountains, and I should get mad at one of my neighbors, I might set a mountain down on his house. Well guess what, that is not going to happen.

Sometimes you may hear preachers say, *"If you ask GOD something in faith, He must do it."* The real truth is GOD answers prayer according to His will, not ours. Suppose you had a loved one who was dying and you begged GOD to keep them alive, and GOD knew they would be a vegetable the rest of their lives, would you want that? I believe the Bible is clear that we should pray for all requests people make to us, but accept GOD's answer when He gives it. I know that sometimes it is hard to give up our wants, and pray for GOD's Will to be done, but it will always work for the best.

Since GOD knows the past, present, and future, and has all power, He could wipe the Earth clean and start over any time He wanted to. That suggests to me that everything GOD does is for the best interest and advancement of mankind. For example, the destruction of Sodom and Gomorrah was actually an act of mercy. The people there had reached a point where they would never turn to GOD at any time in the future. Little babies would have been born with no hope of eternal life because of that influence. So you see, we are just not able to know such things. If we will use the knowledge and wisdom we have received, and let GOD take care of His own business, I think we will be much happier people.

BOTTOM LINE: When Jesus calls His Church up to meet Him in the air that is going to be the grandest homecoming that has ever been. I have a few folks I want to see when I get there.

Your Notes & Scriptures:

18 – GIVING GLORY TO GOD

I am in the waiting room at an auto repair shop. Since my computer is not connected to the system at home, I can't get on the Internet. So I may have to come up with something out of my head. Since my head is almost empty, I may not have much to say. The mechanics say it may take two and a half to three hours to do the maintenance on the van, so I have some time on my hands. Now what in the world can I do with that much time? I can sit here and type on this computer, or think about good things, or do nothing, or go around and pester everyone here in the waiting room. Since most people don't like that very much, maybe that is not such a good idea.

Let me see, I could write a song, or make up a story, or think about things past, or play games on this computer, or watch television. Now, if I write a song I will have to have a subject. What could be the subject of a good song today? If I make up a story, what could it be about? If I think about things past, should I think about the good things or think about all of them? It is so hard to use up time these days when you have nothing to do for three hours. Still what if I could think of something constructive to do? I know what I will do; I will start thinking about the next devotional column for the newspaper. The column will have to be something that GOD can use for His purpose, something that will not glorify mankind, but show His own glory and grace.

Actually, as I sit here and start to think about it, GOD's glory is shown in everything we can see around us.

When He made the world, He put everything in and on it that mankind would ever need. I believe GOD's purpose for creating humans, was to have fellowship with them. I believe that purpose has not changed. If we want to melt GOD's heart we should have a desire to be close to Him and obey His commands. Jesus said that His *"yoke is easy and his burden is light."* The Devil would have us believe that if we become a Christian, we will be under a cruel taskmaster and not allowed to enjoy life at all. That does not make any sense because GOD offers grace and forgiveness for our sins and eternal life in His kingdom. What else can GOD offer to us? I am sure that all of the riches and wealth existing will be in GOD's new Heaven and Earth for us to enjoy for eternity.

BOTTOM LINE: Suppose we just stop thinking negatively and enjoy what GOD has given us here in this life and eternal life later.

Your Notes & Scriptures:

19 – HIDING OUR SINS

We cannot hide from SIN. We cannot hide our own SIN. The Bible is very clear in saying we cannot hide anything from GOD. All of our deeds, words, and thoughts are carefully recorded in GOD's Book. When we are *saved* and become Christians, all our past sins are blotted out. The problem is, we still are prone to sin after conversion. GOD has committed Himself to forgive all our sins for life, but we will pay a penalty for our later sins.

For example, if we eat so much sugar that our teeth rot out, GOD will forgive us for eating the sugar, but he will not make us a new set of teeth; the Dentist has to do that. If we sin until our health is ruined, GOD will forgive us the sin, but He will not restore our bodies back to the original state. You see, sin has a price to be paid. Sometimes we think that because GOD does not punish us right away, we have gotten away with it. Well, as many learned men have stated, we do not get by with it.

All of the Biblical record states that our Lord and Savior Jesus Christ now sits at the right hand of GOD to intercede for us. That means when we are accused of sin before GOD the FATHER, Jesus is right there to say, *"Charge that to me, I paid for it. That person is MINE."* Folks, that is the greatest and most beautiful hope we have. What all this means is, when GOD makes a commitment, it cannot be changed or altered because He is the highest KING. All of the record we have is recorded in the Bible which, when we read it, should cause us to strive to get closer to GOD and sin less. Since we do have the Bible record, that should encourage us to study more and learn what our GOD is doing in Heaven and in this world. I have learned that when I study my Bible, my favorite sin seems to fade. The Devil will not waste any time in bringing it back into my mind, but each time that happens the sin seems to grow more distasteful. I wonder if that means that I should study my Bible every day?

GOD is interested in the least thing that comes our way every day. He is not there to be a taskmaster, but to be our helper and guide. We need to realize that God is a Gentleman. He will not interfere with our activities unless we invite Him to do so. I am sure when GOD sees some of our daily goings, He is saddened by our foolishness.

BOTTOM LINE: We *must* learn to take responsibility for our own actions.

Your Notes & Scriptures:

20 – SET YOURSELF FREE

Many people wake up in the morning with a heavy load of things to worry about, but there is a better plan for Christians. When we wake up in the morning, we should gather up all the worries we have and ask GOD to take them for one day. When the day is over, He can give them back, if He wants to. Sometimes, we want GOD to give them back because we want to keep them for a little while. We feel more comfortable sometimes, when we have something to worry about. One of our worries is, we feel like sinners before GOD and we judge ourselves instead of letting GOD do it. Jesus said that He did not come to call the righteous, but sinners to repentance.

Receiving Jesus Christ as our personal Savior does not mean we will not sin for the rest of our lives. We still have the old sinful nature, and will give in to temptations sometimes. GOD knew that and provided forgiveness for sin for the rest of our lives. That does not give us a license to sin anytime we want to, but we are to grow in grace and become as much like Jesus as possible. We get our *want-to* fixed. Going back into sin makes us worse than before we were saved, because we have been enlightened by the Holy Spirit and do not have an excuse to sin against GOD anymore.

Another worry or responsibility that we have is seeing to the safety of ourselves, our families, and those who we may encounter in our daily activities. For example, an automobile usually weighs between 3000 and 4000 pounds. If we get careless and hit another car, the impact could be like a small bomb, and do great damage, or kill someone. Our cars are our own responsibility, and GOD will hold us accountable for the misuse of them.

Another worrisome thing is when we reach that point in life when we are no longer bullet-proof and cannot leap tall buildings at a single bound. I never thought I would reach that point, but the sad truth is; I did. Well, enough foolishness, let's move on.

BOTTOM LINE: "Lord, grant me the serenity to accept the things I cannot change, the courage to change the things I can, and the wisdom to know the difference. AMEN."

Your Notes & Scriptures:

21 - A LETTER TO THE EDITOR

A church member wrote a letter to the Editor of a newspaper and complained that it made no sense to go to church every Sunday.

"I've gone for 30 years now," he wrote, "and in that time I have heard something like 3,000 sermons, but for the life of me, I can't remember a single one of them. So, I think I'm wasting my time and the preacher is wasting his by giving sermons at all."

This started a real controversy in the *Letters to the Editor* column. Much to the delight of the editor, it went on for weeks until someone wrote this clincher:

"I've been married for 30 years now. In that time my wife has cooked some 32,000 meals. But, for the life of me, I cannot recall the entire menu for a single one of those meals. But I do know this... They all nourished me and gave me the strength I needed to do my work. If my wife had not given me these meals, I would be physically dead today. Likewise, if I had not gone to church for nourishment, I would be spiritually dead today!"

BOTTOM LINE: When you are DOWN to nothing....God is UP to something! Faith sees the invisible, believes the incredible and receives the impossible! Thank GOD for our physical AND our spiritual nourishment!

Your Notes & Scriptures:

> "Our scientific power has outrun our spiritual power. We have guided missiles and misguided men."
>
> — Martin Luther King, Jr.

22 – THE GREATEST BATTLE GROUND

The greatest Battle Ground in all history, where the most furious and deadly battles have been fought and are still being fought, is the human mind. After the fall of mankind, the battle for control of all human minds has been fought by GOD and Satan. GOD's goal is to save as many as will believe in Him and accept His Son Jesus Christ as their personal Savior. Satan's goal is to destroy as many people as he can by keeping them from accepting GOD's plan of salvation for their souls. Any human who wants to take a look, can see both kinds of people. Those following Satan are out of control for the most part. That does not mean that they are all bad people, but they have just rejected GOD's call to salvation. Christians, on the other hand are trying to serve GOD and live according to His instructions; the Bible, at least, they should be.

Refusing to trust GOD for salvation, and living for Satan, means a person can live their live on this Earth with all the existing problems, and at the end of life, go into the fire in Hades. *(The following explanation of Hades and Heaven is my own thoughts, and not written in any book).* When a lost person dies, their soul is released from the body and simply goes down into the center of the Earth where the fire burns continually. The fire there is not a consuming fire; it burns only on the sins the person has committed in their lives. That means that it burns on the inside and cannot be put out. The person receives a temporary body which can feel pain, can see, hear, talk, and feel remorse. That is called the *second* death. In my thinking, that means that person dies continually for eternity. A few of the lost who have experienced a moment of that pain, say that it is many times worse than any pain on this Earth.

When a true Christian person dies, their soul also comes out of the body and is *carried* by the angels into Heaven where they also receive a temporary body which can be recognized by those who knew them on Earth. There they will rest until the Lord Jesus Christ comes back to Earth with His saints. At that time the dead in Christ will come out of their graves and all saints will receive their new glorified bodies. We are not told all that will take place at that time, but we will all be with our Lord and Savior Jesus Christ.

BOTTOM LINE: The battle for control of our minds is a serious one and can bring eternal death to the lost and can bring a ruined life for the Christian. However, the Christian has another choice. Obeying GOD and following His directions, written in the Bible, bring Joy and peace from GOD Himself. Obeying GOD is our very best choice.

Your Notes & Scriptures:

23 – GETTING ATTENTION

It seems all humans have a burning desire to be recognized and make some kind of mark in their generation. The attention we crave must start at home while we are growing up. If children cannot get attention at home, they will find it someplace else; *usually in the wrong place*. Lately, some have been stealing cars and giving the police a high speed chase which endangers the lives of several people. This is just an example of how desperate young people are to get attention from someone, although they know what the final end will be. There are many other examples, like when someone runs out onto the pro baseball field while the game is going on, knowing they will be caught and arrested.

Most of us are pretty clever in hiding our way of getting attention, or at least we think we have it hid. There is one thing we should remember we cannot hide our secrets from GOD. I believe GOD longs to give us the attention we long for, but He will only do it His way. The Bible is very clear that the person who will submit to GOD's will and humble their heart will be lifted up. What that means is, God will vindicate us when we follow His will. GOD will lift us up before the world so we may be effective in what we do. But when we start taking the credit ourselves, GOD will take us to His *woodshed*. Now, I can tell you for a fact, you will not like GOD's woodshed.

It appears that all mankind receives some kind of talent at birth to use in making a living for their families. Have you ever wondered why some people will be policemen and policewomen and just will not be happy doing anything else? The Bible says that GOD sustains His creation and that is one way He does it. The other talent GOD may give when we accept Jesus Christ as our personal Savior is to be used in His service. GOD would not give a lost person the talent to preach the Gospel or serve in His Church.

When we submit to GOD's will and get into His service, He will provide the joy and peace that Jesus promised, however if we start saying, *"Look what I have done,"* we are headed for trouble. GOD has never shared His Glory with anyone. All down through the ages the Devil has tried to use people to claim part of GOD's glory. It has never worked, and it never will.

BOTTOM LINE: GOD given attention is beautiful. Self gotten attention is ugly.

Your Notes & Scriptures:

24 – DOUBTING GOD

YOU CANNOT DOUBT SOMETHING YOU NEVER HAD.

Doubting our beliefs and believing our doubts seems to be common among many Christians. Each time we go through some trial or rough spot, we start thinking GOD has kicked us out because we are so bad. If GOD really did that, none of us could survive. One thing I have learned is, when GOD makes a commitment it is unchangeable. I believe that is the reason GOD wants us to grow to be like Him. We need to learn how important it is to make our word good, and take GOD at His Word that He will do the same.

Doubt is a killer. Doubt can cause all kinds of troubles in our lives and the lives of people around us. Remember the record of Peter walking on the water to go to Jesus? I think he actually took a few steps on the water before he took his eyes off of Jesus. Then Jesus said, very tenderly, *"Why did you doubt."*

Our Lord Jesus Christ spent hours, days and years trying to build faith in his disciples. He worked with them patiently urging them to trust Him without doubt. Well guess what, Jesus is still working on us today through His Word under the direction of the Holy Spirit to help us to grow into mature Christians. I wonder how many of us are still acting like small school Children.

Serving GOD daily is not for wimps. Satan can take all the wimps and chew them up and spit them out into the river of sin and over the waterfall of ruin. It is very easy to make a mistake, but it is so hard to recover from it.

Jesus said to his disciples that they would have many trials and troubles in this world but to be of good cheer, because He has overcome the world. It seems to me that Jesus wanted His children to rely on Him to take care of their problems that they could not handle. It seems to make sense that if we take care of our portion of GOD's business that He will take care of our troubles while we are in the world. I heard the story of one of GOD's ministers who worried continually about his kids getting to go to college. Then one day GOD told him plain that he should take care of his preaching and leave the college kids up to Him (GOD).

    I believe GOD would have us to have a mind-set about serving Him in our place and leave the worrying up to Him. One thing we should never forget is that GOD's plan is in motion and nothing is going to hinder or stop it. We may not like it, but it is His plan.

    BOTTOM LINE: Let's just start believing our beliefs and stop doubting our doubts.

Your Notes & Scriptures:

25 – AMERICA'S CONSTITUTION

THE CONSTITUTION OF ANY COUNTRY OR STATE IS ONLY AS GOOD AS THE PEOPLE WHO WROTE IT.

These are a layman's thoughts and comments about the original intent and writing of the laws and regulations governing our country, the United States of America. At first the country had just been in a bloody war to gain independence. There were only a few states at first, and each one had their own Constitution. A few wise men, mostly Christians, saw that if America was to be a united country, there would have to be a government set up by all the states to regulate and serve all the people.

But, it still had to give the states the freedom to maintain their own government with their own elected officials. A few wise and dedicated men began to write up the rules and regulations that would become the United States Constitution. It took several years to finally construct a document that all the people would and did approve. By these rules and regulations, each state would elect a number of officials to represent them in the capitol of the country.

The government was set up to have three units of equal authority to vote on the issues that came up, namely the Legislative Branch, the Judicial Branch, and the Executive Branch. To make a long story short, each one of these *elected* officials serves a certain number of citizens who elected them by vote. It is my understanding that these three branches were set up to serve the people and not to rule over them. So, what has happened?

Rumors are flying that the United States is nearly bankrupt. Elected officials have made laws to exempt themselves from some of the rules and regulations, which were not approved by the people. GOD is being kicked out of society, many Christians are getting cold in their faith, and we may now be in danger of losing some of our most precious liberties. I don't mean to paint a picture of doom and gloom, but our future does not look so bright just now.

From the Christian viewpoint, suppose the *times* fit into GOD's plans for making an end of time, as we know it. He does not need our approval to finish His plans. Many of the problems of today are seen in the prophecies of the Bible for the end times. I am not saying that we should do nothing, but we should accept the things we cannot change and thank GOD that we are closer to *going home* than we were yesterday.

I believe and am sure that the rapture of the Church is not far away. No one knows when it will be, but Jesus said that when we see the signs spoken of in the Bible, to look up for the rapture is near.

BOTTOM LINE: GOD knows all the answers and has everything well in hand, so we would be wise to draw closer to Him and let Him do the worrying for us.

Your Notes & Scriptures:

26 – REPENTING OF OUR SINS

HOW OFTEN SHOULD I REPENT OF MY SINS AND TURN BACK TO GOD?

That is a good question that must be answered by each Christian. After thinking about it, I believe we should repent of our sins and turn back to GOD as often as we sin. Being *human* and living in such a sinful world makes it hard to stay close to GOD all the time. The best part about GOD is, when He makes a commitment it cannot be changed or altered. I believe GOD wiped away our past sins when we were *saved* and then made a lifetime commitment to forgive all our future sins, although our future sins are costly and damaging to our lives.

It seems that all of the *seeds* I have allowed to come into my mind, good or bad, can be called back by GOD at any time, but they can also be called back by the Devil at any time, in fact the Devil can call back a deed we have done against GOD and say, *"Remember what you have done? GOD cannot use you for holy and spiritual work because you are just a sinner."* That is just one of the things Jesus warned us about in His Word. That's why He urged us to place our faith in Him.

When Jesus was on the Earth, He placed a high value on faith because faith is our shield against the attacks of the Devil and his demons. Because Jesus wanted us to live out our lives on this Earth and help add to, and build His Church. Jesus knew that without faith we would have no chance to resist the Devil and his host. Faith helps us get up Sunday morning and go to Church to get a spiritual bath and refreshing of the Holy Spirit, with which we can make another week of Christian living. Though the world does not think so, Christian living is the only to go. The joy we get from fellowship with other Christians cannot be found anywhere on this Earth.

Reaching Christian maturity must mean that in spite of the clever devices and temptations the Devil throws our way, we will stand boldly and witness to a lost and dying world. I was not so concerned about reaching out to the world's multitudes with the Gospel until I started hearing about many millions of people who have never even heard of Jesus Christ and His saving power. For example, suppose you were watching a football game with a full stadium and the Church was called up at that moment, how many do you think would be taken up to meet the Lord in the air? Somehow, I think the game would go right on with no notice of missing people.

BOTTOM LINE: Maybe we should not shut up the Gospel we carry around with us, but spread it over our neighborhoods.

Your Notes & Scriptures:

27 – CHRISTIANS' POWER

QUESTION: How much power does a *born-again* Christian have in this life?
ANSWER: None.
QUESTION: How much power is *available* to a *born-again* Christian?
ANSWER: All the power in the universe.

The power we are talking about is the power to overcome temptation, to witness to other people, to live a Christian life, and any other thing GOD may want us to do. While GOD has made His power available to us through the Holy Spirit, He has not given us control of it. We still live in a sinful world, and in a sinful body. GOD says, *"The Spirit is willing but the flesh is weak."* That means that within ourselves we do not have the power to live in GOD's will.

I know that our pride and egos get in the way, but we might just as well face it, we just do not have the power to serve GOD. Sometimes I find myself saying today I am going to do something good for GOD and He will be impressed. Later I find myself laying flat of my face in failure. So I have to ask GOD for another start. It looks like sooner or later I would learn to just check in for duty each morning.

When I was teaching Sunday School, I would often come up with a hum-dinger of a lesson to present to the class. I would feel so good about it that I would almost pop some buttons off my shirt. Then I would find out later that it was a flop. Once again I would have to go back to GOD and repent and get back on track. You see, GOD knows what needs to be said on that certain Sunday, and who needs to hear it. So when I give up myself and my thinking, GOD will come and teach the lesson through me.

Years ago I saw a sci-fi movie which has stayed with me through the years. This race of beings created a giant machine with the power to produce anything they could think of since their brain waves were connected to it. All they had to do was want something and it would appear. At first it worked great until they started getting mad at each other. Their angry thoughts would slip into their sub-conscience mind and while they slept their sub-conscience would call up a monster to kill their neighbor. Years later another race came and found the machine but the whole population had been destroyed. I'm afraid if GOD should trust us with His power, we would all be destroyed like that.

BOTTOM LINE: let me tell you what: Maybe we ought to do our best with what we have and leave everything else to GOD. He can handle it.

Your Notes & Scriptures:

28 – MOVING GOD OUT

When GOD is expelled from any nation, country, state, city, or home, His Word, and principles go with Him. Since the absolutes of virtue and integrity are found only in the Bible, which is GOD's Word, it would be a grave mistake to throw Him out of our country. The reason is, the original Constitution was based on GOD's laws, found in His Word. The great men who wrote the Constitution of the United States determined that without virtue and integrity no people can govern themselves. Freedom cannot be maintained without those virtues, because when people become ungodly and evil they have to have a ruler instead of a leader. I cringe at the idea that our country may be headed in that direction.

How did this happen to our country? One example is, at the time of the writing of our Constitution England was paying high salaries to the men who held government positions. As a result many corrupt men gained those positions by conning the people with great swelling words. *Doesn't that sound familiar today?* Many of the original leaders of our country accepted no salary at all, and the ones who did, did not have any other means of support. I believe they did that to set an example for what is required for a government of a free people to continue to exist and maintain a free country.

The original leaders of our country also realized that future leaders must be trained and prepared for service in the government. They immediately made it clear to all the people that their children must be educated and instilled with virtue and integrity. So it was recommended that the Bible be taught in all schools and colleges. They knew it would maintain a high level of confidence and well- being in the children. We can see it all around us. The children, whose parents have spent lots of quality time with them, are much more apt to stay away from the bad stuff in schools and on the streets.

For all who are true born-again Christians; let's be sure we do our civil duties and rejoice as we see the day coming near when GOD will call us up into the air to meet Him. That is going to be the grandest time any of us can imagine. I remember that my dad had a *five gallon hat;* he couldn't afford a ten-gallon. I wonder if He is still wearing that hat. He would hardly ever go outside without it. Anyway, I am really looking forward to that day.

BOTTOM LINE: I pray that GOD will give us the courage to maintain our Christian walk and strength to endure until the end.

Your Notes & Scriptures:

29 – CATASTROPHIES

How many more *catastrophes* will it take for America to realize that GOD is still in charge even though many people are trying to kick Him out of our country? Sometimes I wonder if GOD is not just amused at the things people try to do. I am sure He is grieved when His own children sit back and do nothing. I think we are all in the same frame of mind when we say, *"Well what can I do about it?"*

Actually our greatest weapon is prayer. Every time I stop and evaluate my prayer life, I am surprised at how little I actually pray seriously about the troubles of our country, church, and my own problems. It is one thing to realize something, and another to take steps to make it right. I can imagine myself doing all those *good* things for GOD and country, so why don't I ever get around to it? One of these days I am going to make everything right, then GOD will be pleased and will bless me a lot; *famous last words.*

As I read those last few lines I noticed a lot of I, me, and myself blessings. I wonder if that may be the biggest problem we have. Lord, I hope I am not the only one with that problem. If I am, somebody ought to shoot me and tell GOD I died. Seriously, we may have more of a *me problem* than we think. It is just possible that we would have to get out of our comfort zone for a little while to make a difference in regaining our country and restoring it back to where it was. We may even have to give up some of our favorite activities in the process.

I really believe that most if not all real Christians would like to be so close to GOD that they could feel His presence 24/7. One thing is for sure, we would have joy unspeakable and full of glory. That thought makes me long for the day when Jesus will call us out of this life and into His presence. We can see some of the signs that Jesus spoke about in His Word already happening before our eyes. That alone should encourage us to face the things that are coming and stand firm in our faith and belief. Tell you what; let's just vote our convictions and support each other, and leave the rest up to GOD. Who knows but what is happening in America is could be part of GOD's plan for the last days.

BOTTOM LINE: Let's just trust GOD to do everything right according to His plan.

Your Notes & Scriptures:

30 – GOD'S TEMPLE TODAY

Suppose a mob of true Christians went into GOD's Holy Temple and began to chop, cut, kick the walls, and beat all the figures to dust until none were left. What do you think GOD would do? Suppose, with that in mind, I were to tell you that many of us are doing just that. I have just learned that some of our *Health Experts* have determined that one of the greatest dangers to our country is us *Couch Potatoes.* They are saying we cost our country billions of dollars in health care alone, including all the medicine we take, some of which is paid for by the Government.

In addition to that, some of us could not handle a weapon if our lives depended on it. And if our military forces were spread all around America, I think they would be a little thin in places. Most of us could not fight off any intruder who endangered ours and our families' lives.

The Bible says that when a person is born-again, the Holy Spirit moves into their soul and their bodies become Temples of the Holy Spirit, meaning God the Holy Spirit, and when we neglect or damage His temple, He is grieved. I forgot how many times I have said, "That's enough, I have had it, I am going to eat right and exercise like I should." At the time I meant it and with a true heart, I set out on the long journey back to full strength and health. Sometimes my plan would last a whole day. Other times it would last a few hours, still other times it would last until lunch. I guess my plans must have fallen on stony ground.

I believe when we grieve God the Holy Spirit, He does not hate us or think of throwing us out. Instead, I think He grieves for us like a father grieves for his children when they make a bad mistake or get into something he warned them about. The thing that is so amazing about GOD is the fact that He has unthinkable mercy and patience toward us. And, He will take us back and make a fresh start for us anytime we will repent and turn back to Him. The bad thing about our mistakes is that the cost is very high. Although GOD will forgive us and take us back, He will not undo the damage we have done. Think about it like this, if we go so far away from GOD that we ruin our health completely, GOD will forgive us, but He will not restore our health. We have to live with it.

BOTTOM LINE: There is great Joy in serving GOD from the heart, but the opposing *evil* forces never sleep and are at work 24/7 to hinder anything we do for GOD.

Your Notes & Scriptures:

31 – HUM-DRUM

When you woke up this morning, did you say *"Good morning Lord."* or did you say, *"Good Lord, it's morning?"* The difference in those two statements may well be caused by what you did just before you went to bed. No matter how our day may go, we still need to *talk* to the Lord before we go to sleep. It seems that sometimes we forget that GOD is a *living* being and our prayers to Him are just as real as sitting there with Him and talking. GOD is listening just like an Earthly father would do. GOD will give us answers in His time, and in His Word, which is written for us so we can study and learn about our future in Heaven.

GOD takes every problem we have seriously and will take steps to help us with it. We should also realize that GOD allows us to grow and mature by and through our trials and problems. That means GOD will not just zap away our troubles. Instead, He will work them out the very best for us. Sometimes, GOD does not answer our prayers in the way we want Him to, but the end result is always what is best for us.

Growing up in the *spirit* world is no easier than growing up in the physical world. I remember times when I was a kid, I thought my parents didn't like me and didn't want me to have any fun. They were always telling me *"NO"* when I wanted to do something that was dangerous or not good for me. Now I am beginning to see that GOD has the same frame of mind for me, and sometimes He does take me to His *woodshed*. I can tell you from experience that GOD's *woodshed* is not much fun. Well, I guess if GOD is going to have to put up with me for all eternity He has the right to train me for it.

When people sit around and talk, it is often fun and sometimes a person can learn something they did not know. Talking to GOD is not like that. You see, when we talk to GOD we are talking to the owner and King of all creation. Through the power of the Holy Spirit we actually appear, in spirit, in GOD's Throne Room before His court. Since GOD is able to see into our hearts, there is no need to try to fool GOD in any way. I believe GOD actually wants to hear the whole truth and the reason we have come to Him in prayer.

I believe GOD is concerned and listens to us just like a father would if one of His kids came to Him with a splinter in their finger. I believe GOD listens and takes care of our needs in the very best way for us.

BOTTOM LINE: We just need to accept His answer and go on with our lives.

Your Notes & Scriptures:

32 – A MADE-UP STORY

This is a *made up* story, meant to remind us of our relationship to GOD. There have been similar stories written which all point in the same direction.

There was once a kingdom with a good king. When a drought came upon the Kingdom, the King decided to levy a tax on his subjects to maintain the castle and pay the soldiers and workers, etc. A certain group of villages banded together to take their goods, such as wheat, gold, silver, and precious stones to the King.

As they traveled along, they passed through a village which had been really hit hard by the drought and was living on a few grains of wheat each day. The traveling villagers had compassion on them and gave them enough wheat to live on until their crops could be grown and harvested. As the group traveled on, they came to village after village that was in great need.

One village had many sick people and did not have the money to send for a doctor. The traveling villagers just could not leave them in such need, so they gave them as much money as they needed. Well, as they went on their journey, before they had gone little more than half way to the castle, they did not have anything left for the King. As they suddenly realized what that meant, they all became afraid to go to the King with empty wagons and purses. The leader of the group arose up and said, all of you go back to your homes and I will go and try to explain this to the King. If I die, so be it, at least the villages will be saved.

As the leader approached the castle his hair on the back of his neck stood up and goose bumps arose up all over his body. He could imagine big solders dragging him to the chopping block to take his head. He took his place in line and waited for his turn to address the King. It seemed like an eternity before his turn came. Finally his turn came and he began to explain what they had done with the goods they were bringing to the King. He fell on his face and began to beg the King to spare the villages and let him pay the price for coming to the castle empty handed. The King arose and pointed his scepter at the village leader and said, "Bring a royal robe, a golden chain, and a gold ring for this man. Put those on him and bring him to sit with me by my throne."

The leader said, "My King I do not understand." The King smiled and said, *"Because you have done this to the least of my subjects, you have done it to me."*

BOTTOM LINE: Loyalty is more precious than all of the King's treasure.

Your Notes & Scriptures:

33 – TAKING CARE OF OUR BODIES

What has GOD made me responsible for? First, I have life and a body to move around with. Just like anything with moving parts, the body requires regular maintenance and care. We also have the responsibility of using our bodies for GOD's service. After becoming a Christian, my body became the temple of the Holy Spirit. The Bible says that if anyone destroys GOD's temple, GOD will destroy them. I don't think this means that we should spend all our time exercising to maintain perfect health, but we should be mindful that GOD the Holy Spirit lives in our bodies 24/7 and we don't need to bring in unholy food and drink.

Second, I have a good home to live in which is comfortable and good enough to invite friends to visit us on occasion. Of course it also requires regular upkeep and repairs which include yard and outside work often.

Third, I belong to the best church in the world and I have the responsibility to support it and serve GOD there for whatever needs to be done. Our church is very important in my life and all other members as well. I believe when we go to church and hear GOD's Word preached, we should feel like we have had a spiritual bath, and are ready to face the world a little longer.

Fourth, I have received talents from GOD to serve Him with. I don't think He intends for us to entertain the world with our talents but to use them in His service. It seems to me that all talents from GOD, when used properly, will help draw other people to Him for forgiveness of sin and eternal salvation.

Fifth, I have received GOD's love and mercy in the form of forgiveness for sin for the rest of my life. Although I sin against Him often, GOD always takes me back when I confess my sin and turn away from it. That is GOD's promise to us and His word cannot be broken. GOD has also given me the freedom of choice, that is, I can do anything I want to. However, we should be aware that sin is not overlooked by GOD and carries a stiff penalty on this Earth.

BOTTOM LINE: We should be satisfied with what we have and just serve GOD.

Your Notes & Scriptures:

34 – TIME

TIME: What is time? Where did it come from? Who started it?

Maybe we need to spend a little *time* analyzing the effect time has on our lives. First of all, we are creatures of time. Actually, the whole creation is regulated by time. Everything related to time is in motion. Since GOD created time and made the creation subject to time, we too are regulated by time. Our bodies are designed to function by time, and live on the Earth. Earth is the only known place where all things are provided for our existence.

When people go into outer space, oxygen, food and air pressure must be carried along for them to live outside of the Earth. Therefore, we must live naturally on the Earth until our death also. Because of the curse of sin we cannot go into Heaven without our bodies being changed to spiritual bodies.

Well, now that our minds are totally boggled, let's go another direction and plant some seeds. We each have 24 hours a day, seven days a week. A poor person has the same amount of hours per day as a rich person. Suppose we put $10.00 value on each hour, which would give us $240.00 each day to invest. Since GOD has given us complete freedom and responsibility for our time, maybe we should pay more attention to our life-style. If we break it down, we will spend $80.00 per day sleeping, more or less. We will spend another $80.00 working, and another $20.00 traveling to and from work. That leaves $60.00 for other things.

Christians believe that the tithe, which is one tenth of our income, belongs to the Lord while we live on this Earth, and should be brought in on a regular basis. However, in the beginning of bringing tithes to the Lord, that included all the possessions of a person or family. Surely *time* would also be included in that category. That means two hours and twenty four minutes would be due each day. There must be several different ways one could spend that time serving the Lord.

One way would be going to Church, and another could be visiting for the Church. Still another could be working around the Church, doing repairs and upkeep. Others would be such things as teaching classes, working with children, preparing food for people recovering from illnesses, visiting people in the hospital, and a number of other things.

I heard this story about an elderly blind lady who had gotten a phonebook with raised letters and numbers so she could find phone numbers. Although she had this phonebook, she was still so depressed she asked the Lord to take her on home to Glory. But GOD asked her what she had in her hand. When she told Him, He said, "USE WHAT YOU HAVE!" So, she began to call people to tell them about Jesus and the plan of salvation. At the end of her life, it was learned that she had called more than 9,000 people.

BOTTOM LINE: Time's a-wasting…get busy!

Your Notes & Scriptures:

35 – PURE FREE CHOICE

Beginning with Adam and Eve, all humans have received the gift of *free choice* from GOD. People have to make choices all day long, from getting out of bed to going back to bed. This is so common with people that hardly anyone pays any attention to it. It is when people become Christian that their attention is drawn to it by the Holy Spirit, which was given at the point of salvation.

The Holy Spirit begins to help us make the choices that are pleasing to GOD and good for us. When we are faced with some temptation, we have the Holy Spirit to guide us in making the right choice. So then, all Christians have the same choice to sin or not to sin. I seem to want to think, "Well I just can't resist this temptation." I have heard of a term that describes that; it is called *Hog-Wash*.

Along with the power of choice comes the power to make GOD-pleasing choices about any temptation that we may face. We should always remember that the Devil was defeated by Jesus at the Cross. He has no power over us at all. He can only tempt us through our minds, using the desires of our bodies (or flesh). However we should never under estimate his power of persuasion. When we start thinking we can handle it, we are headed for a hard fall.

To make a long story short, sin is sin. We sin by choice, we gossip by choice, we hate some people by choice, we miss church by choice, and so on, and so on. I find that when I do make the right choice sometimes, it makes the wrong choice seem so small and ugly, also it seems to make the next choice easier to make right. I do believe GOD would have us to stand up and make good choices for His glory and our growth in our Christian Spirit.

    BOTTOM LINE: Resisting temptation, making right choices, and serving GOD on Earth may not be easy. But I have been told that the benefits are outstanding, and the retirement plan is out of this world.

Your Notes & Scriptures:

36 – THANKFUL

What do you do when you can't think of anything to say to GOD or anything to ask for? You want to talk to Him, but nothing will come out of your mind or heart that sounds right. That might be a good time to stop and just say, *"Thank you Lord."*

"Thank you Lord for giving me life. You had my name in Your Book before the world was ever created. I had nothing to do with it. Well, you know what; I don't have much to do with keeping it either. It can be lost in a split second. Frankly, I believe if You pull back Your hand for only a moment, the Devil will snuff it out. When I was saved and my name was recorded in the Lamb's Book of Life, I still didn't have any power to keep myself. So, thanking you for giving me life and keeping it for me is appropriate.

"Thank you for allowing me to be born in the United States of America. It was, and still is the best country in the world. The freedom we enjoy in this country is better than anywhere else. For example, as long as I have the money and don't break any laws, I can travel anywhere in this country without being arrested or harassed by any authorities. I can go shopping when I please, I can go on a vacation when I please, and many other things.

"Thank you that I can still go to any church I choose and worship in any manner I wish. I can pray, praise, sing, or just listen to the Gospel message being preached by a minister that you choose to proclaim Your Word. I can agree or disagree with him without being beaten or stoned

to death. I can enjoy fellowship with my Christian brothers and sisters. I can hear a message that seems to be meant for me each Sunday. I should go home feeling like I have had a spiritual bath.

"Thank you that I am allowed to own property, to have money in the bank, and to enjoy the best lifestyle in the world. Sometimes, I feel ashamed when I see all that I have and still find something to complain about. Sometimes You must think I act like a big fat kid that sits in his Daddy's lap all day. I remember when I was little; it seemed like when my dad would open the door to come in, a bunch of little mouths would fly open.

"There aren't enough words in our dictionaries to thank You like we should, but I ask You to accept what is in our hearts when we pray."

BOTTOM LINE: Spend time being grateful and thanking God for all of His provisions you enjoy in your life.

Your Notes & Scriptures:

37 – SLOW DETERIORATION

This is a speculative review of some of the past events that have shaped our society up to today. The purpose is to help us understand more about why things are like they are now.

First, during World War 2, young women and young men, *too young to go to war*, went to work in the factories making war supplies. Some were a little older but was exempted from going into the service for one reason or another. These workers made good money, more than they had ever made. They had good places to live and worked their shift each day and went home and enjoyed the time off. When the war was over, most of the factories quit building war machines and started making other things such as cars, washing machines, and all kinds of personal supplies for the American public.

The workers did not want to go back to the farms and suburbs where they barely made a scant living. So, many stayed on at the factories and enjoyed a very good standard of living. As their lifestyle got even better they began to want all the good things they found in the market place, like houses, cars, clothes, and other attractive things.

As their lifestyle got even better, and they began to want more *things*, their lifestyle began to cost more than one person could earn at their jobs. This caused both parents to have to work to maintain that lifestyle. That seemed to be the opportunity the Devil was waiting for. That was the beginning of the destruction of the American family. The Devil began to influence the children's undeveloped minds and cause them to rebel against their parents. Although some parents still disciplined their children, most of the children were without supervision. More often than not, the children would *hang out* together and learn from each other. It does not take a rocket scientist to figure out what that would lead to.

There is an old saying that if you want a child to be bad, do nothing. It is automatic for children to rebel and do what they want to do. The result was turning to something for a little excitement, like dope, fighting, stealing, forming a gang and rebelling against the law. Every time a gang was formed in one town, a gang would form in the next town for their own protection. I have heard it said that over 150,000 young men are in gangs in Los Angeles alone. Many towns now have places in them where it is unsafe to walk down the street. WW2 happened in the 1940's, and some of the second generation following the war, are now serving in the government in Washington.

There has been a decline in morality in the United States from the 1940's to today. I do need to make it clear that this does not include all of the people, but those who did not have supervision in their early lives. As that generation grew up, they never stopped looking for something to bring some excitement into their lives. Soldiers, back from the war saw more horrible things in their service time than most people do in a life time. They too needed some excitement in their lives. We should remember the most physical needs of that sort are supplied by the evil forces. We should also remember that

GOD does *not* supply the physical wants that cause us to sin and turn away from Him.

Speculation: The Devil saw that this generation, and soon the whole country, was turning into a smorgasbord for him and his hoard of demons. They sprang into action and started bringing many things into society such as LSD and other types of dope to further weaken and destroy people's minds. He started alcohol flowing like water all over the country. Most *upper crust* people call it *social drinking*.

When greedy people saw how much money could be made from selling dope and other things to the public, many people become dope peddlers and made lots of money doing it. That caused many young people and adults alike to become *hooked* on drugs for life. Instead of trying to stop it, authorities began to start up Rehab Centers, *band aids*, to try to bring people back to normal.

From then on, each generation became worse than the last one. In the late 1950's and 1960's the *hippy movement* came along. Kids began to get *funny haircuts*. Some parents fussed a little bit, but let it go and went on about their busy lives. Many babies were born of women who were dope addicts and some had defects.

During those early years, a young man walked into a bank and asked for a loan for several million dollars. The banker asked him for his collateral, the young man handed him a magazine called Playboy. The banker looked at it and realized that men would spend lots of money to get one of those magazines, so he loaned him the money. Soon *Playboy Clubs* were built all over the world. The workers in these places discovered they could paint the girls to make them look perfect from head to toe. That is only one of the temptations men face from day to day. The Devil also knew he could take this a step further so he began to slip small amounts of porn into the TV programs, including commercials. Today we have the internet.

BOTTOM LINE: We should never underestimate the power of the Devil. So, hang in there. If you are a Christian, you cannot lose no matter what happens in this world.

Your Notes & Scriptures:

38 – GOSSIP

GOSSIP: What is it? Where does it start? Is it a sin? Does it do any damage?

Gossip is, adding your own words and thoughts to someone else's story or information they may tell you. Example: A teacher once did an experiment with her class of about twenty students. She told the first student that *"John loves Mary."* That student was to tell the next one and the second student tells the next student and so on until all of them had heard it. By the time the story had gone around the class, the story was so bad, *filthy*, it could not be repeated in the company of other people. That does not necessarily mean that the kids were bad, but it meant they were human. I'm afraid that we all have a problem keeping our own thoughts and words out of someone's story.

Another place Gossip may start is when we see someone do something strange or something questionable. Then, we figure it out for ourselves and start telling the news around about what that person did, although we may not know the *real* reason the person did that.

Example: *This is a made up story to make a point.* Once upon a time a group of teen boys learned that the human tongue is a powerful weapon when used wrongly. They decided to pull a prank on one of the ladies in town, who was a school teacher and a Christian lady. They first started telling things about her that was not true. Next they borrowed a pickup truck and parked it in front of her house and just before dawn one of them hid in the hedge and when the neighbors came out to get their papers, he slipped in the pickup and drove away with the lights off. The neighbors did not waste any time passing that information around town.

Soon her church heard the rumors and brought a case against her. Many of the town folks enjoyed chewing on that juicy gossip and soon she was called a scarlet woman and asked to leave the church. To make a long story short, this prank cost the lady her Job, her home, and her standing in the neighborhood. Soon she moved in with her grandparents up north, and was later killed in a farm accident.

If this had been a real story, these boys would get by with it on Earth, but when they stood before GOD the charge would be *"first degree murder"*. Likewise, we cannot know what damage our words might do to someone else and that is why we should be sure our facts are true when we speak to somebody else.

The Bible makes it very clear that we are responsible for every word we speak and goes on to say that we *"will give an account to GOD"* for all of them.

BOTTOM LINE: I had rather be careful now than face GOD later.

Your Notes & Scriptures:

39 – THE DEATH, BURIAL AND RESURRECTION OF JESUS CHRIST

I would like to offer my personal interpretation of the events that took place just after the death, burial, and resurrection of Jesus Christ and the coming of the Holy Spirit.

First: All of the Jews and most of the nations thought that *THE CHRIST* was going to come and restore the nation of Israel and set up His Kingdom immediately. The Jews, over the years since the law was given to Moses, had added so much to the law that Jesus had to spend about three plus years teaching His followers and getting them straightened out with the real truth.

Even after Jesus' teaching and demonstration of His power and authority, the Jews still believed He would restore the Kingdom at any minute. On the day He ascended, they asked if He was going to restore the Kingdom then. He told them they were not supposed to know when that was going to happen.

The Day of Pentecost came and that same day, over three thousand people were saved at the preaching of Peter and the other apostles. Even after the Church was started that day, they still all thought that Jesus was coming back very soon. So all of the converts felt safe in selling all they had to feed all the saints until that time came.

As the Church grew, some say to about 50,000, their supplies began to run out and they did not have anything left to survive on. I believe that GOD allowed them to stay together for time enough to reach all of the

Jews and the other people there. Then GOD allowed severe persecution to come upon them to scatter them to all parts of the country. As they went, they spread the Gospel everywhere. Maybe if we all thought Jesus was coming soon, we would be more willing to help spread the Gospel here.

Over 2,000 years have passed since that time and we have really progressed. We have so many excuses to just stay in our comfort zones and maintain our good lifestyles. After all, GOD gave us what we have and surely He wants us to enjoy it. All we have to do is explain all that to GOD and see what He says. Seriously, I believe that very often we fall victim to our own success. Only a few Christians are filthy rich, but most of us are a little *dirty*.

BOTTOM LINE: We cannot serve GOD if we don't know how. We will not know how until we are willing to grow in GOD's grace and mature in GOD's Word. That will require some sacrifice on our part. That is, we may have to spend more time reading the Bible, and praying for grace and wisdom to stay in the plan GOD has for us. We can't get *glad* until we get mad and sin not.

Your Notes & Scriptures:

40 – GOD GIVEN TALENTS

What am I doing with the talents GOD has entrusted me with?

If I can sing, am I singing? If I can play an instrument, am I playing it? If I can build things, am I building anything? If I can lead people, am I leading? If I can encourage people, am I doing that? If I can show compassion on people, am I showing it? If I can just make a phone call to brighten someone's day, am I doing so? If I can give to GOD above my tithes, am I doing that?

The list goes on and on. It seems that sometimes we forget that GOD does not give out talents for us to keep and enjoy for ourselves. They are given to invest and increase while we are in this world. The purpose of GOD giving us talents is to advance His Kingdom. That can be done by use of any one of the talents mentioned above and many more not listed here. When we develop the talents we are given they become an asset that GOD can use through us to win people to Himself.

If Jesus Christ comes back today or one thousand years from now, His plan is the same and will not be changed. GOD is the only one that really knows the horror of eternity in the *lake of fire* without Him and He does not want anyone to have to go there. So He has given us everything we need to win the lost to Him. He has provided a simple easy way for people to come to him through Jesus Christ, but the problem is that lost people are spiritually dead and cannot hear GOD's call. Our job is to carry GOD's plan of salvation to them where the Holy Spirit can use the Word, GOD's Word, to convict their hearts and lead them to a saving knowledge of Jesus Christ. GOD wants every person to be saved who will accept Jesus Christ as their personal Savior and trust Him for eternal life.

I believe the talents that GOD gives to each of His children are very precious to Him and are the exact ones that each Christian needs. I also believe that when we spend time developing those talents, GOD is pleased and will give us all the courage we need to use them at any time the opportunity comes our way. If we enjoy doing things with our friends here, think how much more we will enjoy doing things with the very GOD of Heaven, when He walks with us on this Earth.

I have heard it said that if one angel was sent to Earth to be president of a large company, and another was sent to sweep the streets, neither one would be jealous of the other or be unhappy with their job. Maybe we should be that way.

BOTTOM LINE: Hang in there.

Your Notes & Scriptures:

41 – DISARMING THE PUBLIC

Do we dare disarm the American public? I have heard that when the Japanese bombed Pearl Harbor the original plan was to come on to the American coast and take enough land to establish a base for them here. The thing that stopped them was that they heard all Americans had guns in their houses. I don't know the source of that story, but it makes more sense than any other reason for them turning back to Japan.

It seems we have a number of people who think that disarming the public would decrease crime in this country. Here are some thoughts along that line. Suppose a group of officials was to go down one side of the street taking up guns from the homes and up the other side doing the same thing. Of course the News Media would be reporting live from the scene. All the public sees this and all the *have-nots* would start thinking, *"This is almost like a city being wide open for looting."* They would not have to fear the people since most home owners are not skilled in combat. So it will be wide open for thieves to break in and steal any time they want to.

Guns *do not* kill people; people do. Almost every *sick-o* that kills people, themselves have a mental problem related to drugs and/or a bad home life. Some people have gone so far as to say that we Americans are killing each other. There is a word to describe that; *Baloney*. I believe and am sure that people who own guns are the most stable people in the country.

Another thought is, giving criminals the same rights as their victims is surely not any deterrent to crime. Some of the criminals live better in prison than outside of it. My opinion along this line is, when a person commits a crime, they forfeit their civil rights until their debt is paid. I believe some of our legal system could stand a little revision.

How does GOD see this problem in America? Would He have us defend ourselves? Or would He have us to just open our doors to the criminals? One thing I remember reading in the Bible is that GOD says to *stand*. I know that is talking about in the Spirit, but would GOD have us to crawl around under foot like a worm? I don't think so. We tend to think our enemies are across the seas, but we have a multitude of enemies around us. Although our worst enemy is ourselves, we do have a great number of physical enemies around us.

BOTTOM LINE: If we hope to do everything right while we are on this Earth, we had better stay close to the source of great wisdom and power; GOD.

Your Notes & Scriptures:

42 – TRUST

TRUST: Trust is a personal *private* belief in the intent and actions of another. For example, trusting GOD to keep His Word and take care of His own. Perhaps the best example of trust is when King David, before he became King, faced a giant that could have been 8 to 10 feet tall with only a sling shot loaded with a stone that he picked up beside a little brook. David also picked up four more stones, because the giant had four brothers and David was ready to face them also if they were there.

David's trust in GOD was so well grounded that he would have faced the whole army if need be. By this record in the Bible, we can see how important it is to trust GOD completely. If we cannot come to a point where we do trust GOD completely, then we often become easy prey for the Devil and his host of demons. Although GOD will forgive our straying and give us a new start, we still lose part of our Christian Joy and fellowship with GOD and our fellow Christians.

Non-Christian people sometimes long to find someone they can trust. In most times they will seek out a Christian first. It makes it very hard if a Christian cannot be found that is trust-worthy. That is sometimes our greatest failing. I know we all live in the same world with the same temptations, but GOD has given us the Holy Spirit for strength to overcome the trials that come our way. Jesus said that He had overcome the world, and in Him, we also can overcome. GOD said He would not allow more temptations to come on us than we can bear.

The beautiful part about trust-worthy Christians is that their spiritual lights shine bright before the world. Those are the ones that are most often sought out when someone is in trouble. I believe letting our spiritual lights shine before the world would surely be a great asset to any community or town. Make no mistake, people do see us when we do anything for GOD, or just go to church.

BOTTOM LINE: The Devil is not going to stand by while we try to serve GOD and each other. The more we get into GOD's work, the harder Satan will fight against it.

Your Notes & Scriptures:

43 – THE LIES WE TELL

The *lies* we tell; how do they affect our relationship with GOD?

LIE: A harsh *untrue* word or phrase that does not sound very good to us *nice* people. The sad truth is we start telling lies from the time we are small children, and actually we never stop. The Holy Bible says, in Genesis Chapter 8, that the thoughts and intent of our hearts are evil from our youth up. Nevertheless, GOD made a covenant with Noah and his family and commanded them to be fruitful and multiply and fill the Earth.

Since that time GOD has worked with people to try to get them to turn to Him for eternal life. GOD has made a way for us to come to Him through His only begotten Son Jesus Christ. We cannot keep GOD's law and make ourselves holy before Him. He had to do that for us. Now GOD says, *"Just call on me and I will save your souls and take you to Heaven when your life is over."*

Problems we face: On Sunday morning your wife walks into the room and asked, *"How do I look this morning?"* Assuming you are a smart Husband, your answer will be exactly what she wants to hear. I am not saying any more about that.

A mother of a new baby asks you how her baby looks. Again, assuming you are smart, that will be the prettiest baby in the whole world. Other problems we face are things that come into our own homes on TV, Radio, and magazines. I think we have been fed this stuff so long that it doesn't seem so bad. That has been going on for years and years. The evil forces we face are strong, clever, and constant day and night, and never ending. If we try to become holy and pure on our own, it would be like trying to walk through a dense jungle without touching any of the leaves on the trees.

Our Christian standing before GOD is His own doing. We actually have no power to overcome evil. GOD has made the way for us and also has promised to keep us through our lives on this world. He made this possible by paying our sin debt in full. That means from our salvation to our death. I know lots of people have a problem with that, but that is the only way it could be. GOD owns everything and controls everything. The Bible says a lot about fearing GOD, but we cannot fear anyone we don't know, actually we have to know *why* we should fear Him by studying His Word and learning more about Him.

BOTTOM LINE: We need to talk to GOD every night and place everything in His hands. When we awake in the morning, we should just *check in* for duty. If we do, our days will go a lot smoother.

Your Notes & Scriptures:

44 – OUR SPOKEN WORDS

Christians; are all of our words *fitly* spoken? Do all of our spoken words glorify GOD? Do all of our spoken words uplift or comfort people? I'm afraid the answer to those questions is *"NO."*

I believe most Christians have a sincere desire to speak in a way that would be pleasing to GOD and man, but the truth is, just as we do not have the ability to pray as we should, but must be assisted by the Holy Spirit, neither can we always speak proper words within the Christian lifestyle. The late Bible teacher J. Vernon McGee said that *what is in the well of the heart will come out through the bucket of the mouth.* Jesus said, we will be justified or condemned by the words we speak. Maybe by growing a little in grace and striving to be more careful when we speak, we might be able to improve the words we speak.

I believe when we speak words to brighten someone's day, or cause someone to laugh even to the point of telling a joke (a clean one), now and then, we are serving a good purpose with our words. When we gossip or tell tales with our words that does not benefit anyone and will degrade other people, we are grieving GOD and bringing shame on ourselves. We will surely be held accountable for those words.

A true Minister of the Gospel of Jesus Christ, Preacher, Teacher, Elder, or any other person sharing the Gospel, must choose their words very carefully. That would mean since we are still human, GOD the Holy Spirit should always be the guide in delivering the message. We should also remember that the enemy of GOD and His Word will strive day and night to dilute the Gospel, or stop it completely.

GOD does not save people and then leave them on this Earth to have a good old time and enjoy everything the world has to offer. Like any Father should, GOD wants His children to grow and learn to be an adult and live like one within the Christian lifestyle, however, before that can happen the new Christian will face many trials and tests from the evil forces. That is what helps us to learn to depend on GOD for the wisdom and strength to overcome the trials. Every time we try to solve our spiritual problems ourselves, we will fall flat on our faces. I should know by now but I always seem to try to serve GOD my way, and solve my own problems. Well I can tell you from experience, it doesn't work.

BOTTOM LINE: Let's just do things GOD'S way.

Your Notes & Scriptures:

45 – THE HOLY SPIRIT

THE HOLY SPIRIT: What does He do? After reading the Bible and listening to many different preachers, here are some of the things the Holy Spirit does.

1. The Holy Spirit came on the Day of Pentecost to indwell the souls of the Christians and put a seal around their souls so they could never again be touched by the evil forces of the world. The Devil can only reach Christians through their minds, but the soul is bought and paid for in full and is safe for all eternity. GOD leaves Christians on this Earth to grow in grace and learn how to serve in GOD's plan.

2. The Holy Spirit gives each Christian certain talents, according to their natural ability. Then He helps to train them to develop their talents and to use them wisely and efficient in GOD's work. Sometimes GOD the Holy Spirit will have a special work for a person to do and will prepare that person before He sends them into the workplace.

3. The Holy Spirit is also the guardian of the Church. I have been told many times that a *Spiritual War* is going on all around us. We cannot see spirits so we are unaware of the *War*, but it makes sense that someone or something would have to stand guard over the Church, else it would surely be destroyed by the evil forces.

4. One of the responsibilities placed on the Holy Spirit is, He is sent to stay with the person He indwells for all eternity. Like any Father, He is grieved when we go off on our *own* thinking we can do GOD's work by ourselves. That also applies to own projects we undertake while

ignoring GOD's help. It seems to me that GOD wants to be involved in our lives and help us to learn to be more like His only begotten Son Jesus Christ, because He is our example for Christian living. Serving GOD is not really a dreaded lifestyle, but is filled with ups and downs, then joy and peace, then ups and downs, then joy and peace, all of which is the way we have of growing in grace. Remember, GOD will *not* allow anything to come upon us that we cannot bear.

    5. BOTTOM LINE: Although the Holy Spirit was not given a name on Earth, He is surely due the same reverence as all members of the GODHEAD.

Your Notes & Scriptures:

46 – PRAYERS WITHOUT WORDS

DOES GOD ANSWER OUR PRAYERS EVEN WHEN WE DON'T SPEAK A WORD?

A TRUE STORY: When my two sons were ages 7 and 9 years old, we got into Midget Car Racing. The little cars had real, 2 Horsepower, engines and ran on a real asphalt track. We could only afford one car, so both boys drove the same car in their age groups. The oldest boy had won several trophies and ribbons, but the youngest boy had never won either one. The track officials decided to give a Consolation Trophy to each boy who had not won one.

The day came and pretty little girls came and presented the trophies to the boys. Most of the boys were elated, but my youngest was not. I came and tried to cheer him up by bragging on his new shiny trophy. He looked up at me and said, "I DID NOT WIN IT!" I had to fight back the tears, (men don't cry). A man and his two young sons also had one car and was doing the same thing that I was doing with my two sons. Both of his sons were very good and won most of their races, which meant that they always got the inside front when the races started.

On this day his oldest son had just finished his race and a strange thing happened. When his car stopped, the oil plug just fell out of his oil case and spilled all the oil onto the track. That meant that his car could not be ready for the next race which my youngest son was in. When the cars were moved to make up for his empty position, my son would be placed on the "inside" front. I could not believe it but I held my breath anyway. I guess my son thought that this was his best chance for fame, so when the race started he put the pedal to the metal and sailed around that track. It looked like that little car was four inches off the track and flying.

Well, to make a long story short, that little boy won his race and drove into the winners circle, and one of the pretty little girls come and gave him his trophy. Then and there he grew from a defeated little boy to a seven foot giant, bullet proof and able to leap tall buildings at a single bound. I was standing back and trying to hold back the tears, but a couple got away from me. I learned a big a lesson that day.

GOD loved that little boy much more than I could ever love him. On that race day, GOD was there waiting at the end of my rope. It is amazing how GOD waits until we exhaust all our plans and attempts to fix things ourselves. GOD truly does look into our hearts for the *real* desires and needs. I know that because I never spoke a word of prayer that race day but GOD was there and fixed things.

Your Notes & Scriptures:

47 – PROCRASTINATION

PROCRASTATION: It seems to have nearly all of us in its grip. We have been given so many things to claim our attention and consume our time, we find it very easy to just sit and enjoy all our TV programs, games of all sorts, computers, and some outside activities. I don't think that we should beat ourselves up because of this but I do think we could channel some of our energy toward serving GOD in these last times.

I have been trying to determine how much I am really concerned about my relatives and close friends concerning their salvation and standing with GOD. Maybe my concern is not as strong as it should be. All I have been hearing from Bible Teachers and scholars suggests that time is growing short with all the world events that are happening.

So if we intend to make a final attempt to reach all those closest to us, we should get started. Praying for those around us is good but it is not enough just to pray. I think face to face contact is the very best way to win people to Jesus Christ. Living a Christian life is also good for the *lost* to see, but it is still not enough to lead people to Christ. If we read about the first church and how they witnessed, we will find that they went house to house spreading the Gospel.

A SUGGESTION: Let's start with the smallest thing that needs to be done and not put it off another second. After that we may be able to get ourselves up and do more things that need to be done. Who knows what that might lead to?

Christians; we are living in a world that is *not* our permanent home. The god of this world, Satan, is using everything he has in his power to disrupt and destroy the witness of the saving grace of Jesus Christ. Since Satan cannot destroy the Word of GOD and the message of salvation, he attacks the messengers. The only way that Christians can carry GOD's Word to the world is through GOD's power. Jesus made it clear when He sent His witnesses out, that they should not try to think of things to say, but would be given words by the Holy Spirit that they should say. If Satan can cause us to use our own words instead of GOD's Word when we witness, he has won the battle and people will not really be saved.

BOTTOM LINE: GOD knows every thought and intent of our hearts and minds. He knows all our plans, our needs, and our wants. Believe it; GOD *will* give us the right words to say when we need them.

Your Notes & Scriptures:

48 – PUSH, PUSH, PUSH

PUSH, PUSH, PUSH! We have to push ourselves every day to get the things done that we need to do. Our great spiritual enemy knows that we don't like to leave our comfort zones for any length of time, so he impresses on our minds that that job or chore is not important and we can just let it slide, or put it off for awhile.

Satan also does the same thing about serving GOD or doing things for other people. Young people live and work in a fast moving world and think they do not have the time to serve GOD and other people. Older people must deal with aches and pains and find it much easier to stay in the recliner with the TV on than to get up and serve GOD and mankind.

So we have to start pushing when we wake up to get ourselves out of bed and into the activities of the day. It seems that GOD is willing to give us the strength and desire to serve Him and His people however. GOD cannot bless our steps if we don't ever take one. GOD cannot be active in our lives if our lives are not active. GOD will not create activities in our lives if we are not willing to accept and use them for His honor and glory. Having said all of that, we should consider the following.

Our GOD does not sit up there in Heaven with a big whip in His hand waiting for one of us to make a mistake. In fact I am convinced that GOD's love for us is so great that He watches day and night for a chance to bless us. I believe GOD longs to hear prayers from us, especially when we admit that we sin against Him every day and desire His forgiveness and fellowship.

If we are willing to develop a strong desire to push ourselves when we need it, I believe we will soon find it easy to start each day. I believe we will grow in grace and fellowship with our GOD and our lives will be much more fulfilled with joy and peace.

BOTTOM LINE: The signs of the times should cause us to be more active in the work of GOD and the activities of our churches. We can see some signs that our lives may be changed soon and many people are not aware or concerned about it. Maybe we should start our days with a prayer and end our days with a prayer.

Your Notes & Scriptures:

49 – THE SECOND COMING

Jesus Christ is not coming back to this Earth to call out His church until He gets ready. No matter how many dates people set, or how many signs come to pass, we are going to have to wait on Him. That seems to be one on the hardest things for us to do. When we ask GOD for something, we want it immediately. Sometimes we may give Him a few minutes, but we won't wait long before we start complaining.

Starting around the 1950's, society started moving faster and faster until now we often stand in front of our microwaves and pat our foot and say, *"hurry, hurry."* I don't know what we think we have to do that we have to rush around so much. Apparently we are trying to flow with the times and not let anyone get ahead of us, although often times we are not really going anywhere or don't have a set time to get there.

Patience is not one of our best virtues. We see the lack of it in us and many of our friends. Although patience is one of the things that GOD loves for His children exercise, it is also one of the hardest things for us to develop in ourselves. The Bible says that patience comes by trials and testing, and we all hate to go through them. Another condition for gaining patience is, we have to want it. But, if we are not in close touch with GOD, we will *not* want it.

When a person develops their patience, it becomes an asset to them and to all the people around them. One of the greatest things about that; the person is able to listen instead of wanting to talk all the time. Many people we know want someone to just listen to them. I believe GOD is well pleased when we are willing to do that. That is when many people's problems can be solved.

BOTTOM LINE: Just listen to GOD and other people. You will be glad you did.

Your Notes & Scriptures:

50 – ONE ROAD TO HEAVEN

One road leads to heaven. All others lead down to the pit called hell *or Hades*. Jesus said, *"I am the way the truth and the life, no man comes to the father except through me."*... PERIOD!

Why is it so hard to believe that Jesus Christ is the only way to Heaven? He left His Throne in GOD's perfect Paradise to live on Earth and die a horrible death, so none of us would have to pay for our sins. While He was on Earth, He spent His three adult years training people in the *true* way of righteousness. Name any other deity who has done that and we will discuss it. A man once asked GOD why it is so hard to follow Him and so easy to follow the Devil. GOD replied, *"Because I have only one way and the Devil has many ways. Also, all of the Devil's ways are downhill, so the traveling is easy and smooth."*

If Christians, living on this Earth, follow GOD completely, they will often have trials and troubles because the Devil hates the very thought of someone following GOD. He even tried to get Jesus to bow down to him by promising to give Him the whole world. If a Christian acts and lives like Jesus Christ, they will be treated like He was. But if we are to do the works that GOD has commanded us to do, that is exactly what will happen. We could think of it as being in enemy territory and trying to serve our government out in the open.

Think how great it will be to stand in the presence of GOD and hear all the wisdom of the universe coming into our ears. The servants of Solomon were always very happy to hear the Wisdom of Solomon as they stood guard in his presence. Think how much greater GOD's wisdom will be. I don't know about you, but I have lots of questions to ask GOD when I stand in His presence.

BOTTOM LINE: When all the final judgments are over, I hope GOD can find a place of service for me somewhere in His Kingdom. It has been hard to serve GOD through the years, and I can't claim to be one of the strong ones, but standing anywhere in GOD's Kingdom will make me rich above anything I could imagine.

Your Notes & Scriptures:

51 – THE HOLY BIBLE-THE BEST BOOK

GET HOOKED ON THE HOLY BIBLE, READ IT ALL THE TIME.

The Holy Bible is a vast storehouse of knowledge. It has the account of the first man and women, how they were made, why they were made, where they lived and GOD's plan for them. I don't know if they had belly buttons or not; (some people have asked that question), it doesn't matter.

The beauty of the Garden of Eden is described in the first few pages of the Bible. GOD's love for those first two people must have been very great. He came and walked with them in the cool of the evening. I wonder what it would be like to walk and talk with GOD side by side. *Christians do walk and talk with GOD, but in a different way*. The Holy Spirit we receive at the point of salvation takes us into the presence of GOD when we make our requests to Him.

The fall of Adam and Eve in the garden is also recorded in the front of the Bible. When GOD made the man Adam and woman Eve, the evil one, the Devil, was there and saw that Eve was made the weaker vessel. He come to her first and tempted her to disobey GOD by eating the forbidden fruit. His plan to bring sin into GOD's creation worked and now all Christians must fight the same battle against the temptation to rebel against GOD and commit sin of some sort.

The Holy Bible is a Treasure Chest of answers to hard questions. Any question a person may have can be found in the Bible. One of the problems we have is, not knowing where to find them. That leads us to the fact that GOD is willing to give His children, Christians, wisdom when they ask for it, but we must get knowledge the hard way; we have to study for it. That is why it is so important to read the Bible daily. Reading the Bible is not a chore, it is a privilege given to us. Over 90% of the Bible is written for Christians, not lost people.

BOTTOM LINE: Our time is consumed by many different things or events. When we attempt to do anything in GOD's service, things from every direction start trying to claim our time. If we put it off too long, the urging spirit will soon cease and we lose that chance to serve GOD forever. Read, Read.

Your Notes & Scriptures:

52 – OBEY THE RULES

OBEY: We have several things we need to obey while we live on this Earth. There are laws, teachers, parents, and a host of others, but the greatest of all is the need to obey GOD. When a person is born again and receives the Holy Spirit, GOD wants to be that person's guide, through the Spirit, day by day. GOD actually puts that person in training for living with Him in eternity.

GOD leaves His Children on Earth to be trained to be like His Son Jesus Christ. If GOD took away all of our troubles and trials each day, we would be big fat spoiled kids, spiritually. By remaining on this Earth, we can learn to deal with people of all sorts and hear all kinds of stories as to why they don't come to the Lord for salvation. We learn to be a witness for GOD to bring as many people to Jesus as possible.

That does not come automatic, we have to study and learn from GOD's Word to take part in His work on this Earth. We need to remember that He did not create Adam and Eve to lay around in the Garden of Eden. He created them to take care of the garden. I think that may have meant for them to prune the plants and trees, and to see that it was growing right.

You see, GOD in His wisdom created our bodies to work, or to be busy. The muscles that operate our moving parts have to be used to stay strong and healthy. All of this would be so easy if we did not have the god of this world tempting us day by day to sin against GOD and break our fellowship with Him. So GOD walked with Adam and Eve before they disobeyed Him and ate the forbidden fruit.

After that, GOD no longer walked with Adam, but talked to him through the Spirit. Today, GOD has fellowship with us through the Holy Spirit He gave us when we were saved. When we listen, and obey, the fellowship is great. When we don't obey, we will surely be taken to GOD's *woodshed* for an attitude adjustment.

Obeying the laws of the land is good, it keeps us out of lots of trouble, but obeying GOD keeps us out of Spiritual trouble. I can tell you for sure, it is not fun to disobey GOD and make Him angry. Oh yes, GOD does get angry with His children sometimes.

BOTTOM LINE: Jesus will instantly save a person that comes to Him in repentance, and He will also take us back into fellowship with Him when we repent of our sins.

Your Notes & Scriptures:

53 – SIGNS OF THE TIMES

What is the sign that tells when Jesus is coming again with His saints?

Actually, there is no sign that tells the day and hour when He will appear in the sky.

After thinking about that and talking to friends and others I come to realize that the signs we talk about are *signs of the times*. As we see the world events taking place today, we believe that Jesus will soon come with His saints and rapture the Church to meet Him in the air. The way I see it, if He does *not* come soon, most of the nations of the world will self destruct because of lust for power, greed, and lack of leadership.

The Bible says that where there is no vision, (qualified leadership with vision), the people perish. America is surely included in that because our leadership is not following the original laws and intent of our foundering fathers. If we are to continue to be a free people, we will have to get back to and follow the Constitution as it was originally written. I don't see that happening in the near future.

What lies ahead for America and its citizens? No one can predict the future, but the signs of the times are tell-tell signs of major events about to take place. *Now* might be a good time to get a little closer to GOD. I think we could all use a little reassurance of GOD's watch care over His children in these perilous times. One thing we know for sure is GOD's plan is still in motion and He is in control of every minute of time. GOD knows all about the condition of the nations around the world and He will make sure that everything happens according to His plan.

BOTTOM LINE: If we have any intent to speak to our lost love ones, kin folks, our friends and neighbors, about the plan of salvation, I think we had better get started while there is still time.

Your Notes & Scriptures:

54 – MANY GODS

HOW MANY *gods* DO WE HAVE IN AMERICA?

Number one may be, **MONEY**. Money is our medium of exchange and the method we use to pay our bills. We all seem to think that if we have lots of it, we will be very happy. I have heard stories of people who won the lottery, and their lives took a change for the worse. Many wish they had never won the lottery. It seems that GOD has given each of us enough to live, and all we can be responsible for.

Land may be next. Many people think that land is the greatest wealth a person can have and they spend their lives trying to get more of it. One person was heard saying that they only wanted all the land that joins their property. Long ago a man tried to buy a piece of land from an old Indian. The Indian said, *"How can you own a piece of land? You cannot take it with you when you move."* Another man once asked a minister if he did not own the land that he had the title to, who does? The minister said, *"Ask me again one hundred years from now."*

Watching **Sports** is one of the biggest activities that keeps people away from GOD and His Church and service. Although there is nothing wrong with playing or watching sports, if it comes before GOD, it becomes a sin and unacceptable to GOD. I believe GOD allows us the freedom to watch or play in any type of sports, if it does not take His place in our Hearts and lives.

Political Power may be another thing people seek more than GOD. I have heard that when a person is elected to certain positions in Washington, they get their full salary, which is huge, for the rest of their lives, plus free medical care. One can see why that would be something to seek after.

Other things that can push GOD out of people's lives may be **Alcohol**. It is legalized around the world and is kept in most households. I doubt that anyone would become an alcoholic on purpose, but most people are unaware of just how addictive it is. They start off to be social with other people, then they like the way they feel after drinking and they drink more and more often. Alcohol is one of the Devil's greatest weapons.

BOTTOM LINE: Beware of the Devil's traps.

Your Notes & Scriptures:

55 – NO DEFENSE

There is no defense against LOVE. GOD loves mankind with unchanging love. That is why people get under convection when they hear the true Gospel preached. The people who heard the message Jesus brought to the world, could not attack the message, so they attacked the messenger; Jesus.

The same thing happens today. People cannot deny the message of the Bible, so they reject the messenger. It is hard to explain the *real* way to Heaven when the listeners are looking for ways to reject it, and claim they know another way. Think about how confusing it would be if there was another way to Heaven. As Christians, we know that there is not, but many people are trying to say there is.

If someone could actually find another way to Heaven, they could then throw out the Bible and would not come under conviction for sins they commit. The true Gospel reveals our sins before a holy GOD. Then we have to repent of our sins and accept GOD's free pardon of our sins and the gift of eternal life, or we have to reject it completely which means to receive *eternal death* away from GOD in the lake of fire. There is no in between, and the two options are certain and *will* come to pass.

GOD created mankind to have fellowship with Him. GOD never meant for Adam and Eve to fail and disobey His command by eating the forbidden fruit. GOD knew that when Adam and Eve gained the knowledge of good and evil, they would not be able to resist the temptation to turn away from GOD and go their own way. We can see that today in young children. They will pull away from their parents and go to do their own thing. The only time they run to the parents is when they get hurt or when danger is close by. It seems that grown-ups do GOD the same way. I know that sometimes when I ask GOD to help me do something and He does, I start thinking, now I know all about this so I don't need GOD to help me anymore. *Big mistake!* When that happens I always go a little ways and then *crash and burn.*

Jesus said, *"Come unto me all you that labor and are heavy laden and I will give you rest, take my yoke upon you and learn of me for my yoke is easy and my burden is light, and you shall find rest for your souls."*

BOTTOM LINE: I can't think of a better promise than that. One thing we know, if we do that, we will be in GOD's will.

Your Notes & Scriptures:

56 – GOD MADE A MAN

    GOD became a man and came to this Earth to seek and save that which was lost. What was it that was lost? Adam and Eve walked with GOD in person while they were in the Garden of Eden. When they disobeyed GOD and ate the forbidden fruit, GOD could no longer walk with them because GOD is so perfect that He cannot even look at sin without degrading His perfect dwelling place. Christians today have fellowship with GOD through the Holy Spirit but not face to face. That is what was lost in the Garden of Eden, GOD's personal fellowship with His creation.

    Jesus had to come to Earth and pay that terrible sin debt before fellowship with GOD could be restored. Since all human flesh is sinful, fellowship can only be restored by saving and sealing the souls of people. GOD chose not to destroy the flesh at the point of salvation but chose to allow the Devil to tempt mankind so mankind could learn to lean on GOD's power to overcome the temptation and enter into GOD'S work here on Earth.

    GOD is able to allow sin to continue on Earth because GOD the Son, Jesus, became a man and could use His blood to cleanse any person who will repent of their sin and turn to GOD for salvation. The grandest part of GOD's plan is that forgiveness is always available for the rest of a Christian's life. No human can save themselves. Neither can any human keep themselves. If we could, we would not need GOD with us all the time.

    GOD's Word, the Bible, is the key to learning how to serve GOD while we live here on this Earth. Every question we might have is answered in the Bible. Also when we try to bring a loved one to Jesus for salvation, the Bible will have to be used to convince them that they are sinners and need GOD's salvation. The plan of salvation is simple but very important. It is simply this: Jesus came to Earth, spent approximately three years teaching men the true Gospel, and then was crucified for our sin debt. He was buried and came back to life after three days to go into the presence of GOD the Father to intercede for us continually. I don't know how it could be any simpler than that. We didn't have to *do* anything.

BOTTOM LINE: Let's stop trying to earn something and just trust GOD with our lives.

Your Notes & Scriptures:

57 – OUR FINAL DECISION

It seems that the time has come to make our final decisions about serving the Lord until the end of our lives. I think that means that the decisions we make now will have to be sure and steadfast until the end. The reason for this kind of thinking, up until now, is that Christians have not really faced any hard trials or temptations concerning our loyalty to GOD and Church. It is very possible that in the near future we may be told what we must do or think along this line.

If we don't settle it now, that we will remain faithful to GOD and His cause, we could find ourselves following along with any *good-sounding* cause that comes along. We should not underestimate the powers of the evil forces. The Devil and his angels are smarter than any person on this Earth. We should always remember that this Devil has nothing to lose because his final end is already determined. As the end time comes closer, Satan will use everything in his power to keep us from doing GOD's will while we live on this Earth.

I don't think GOD would have us to drop everything and try to serve Him 24/7. But I believe He would have us to be stronger in our faith as we go about our daily lives. Since our lives should belong to Him anyway, being faithful to our Lord and Savior Jesus Christ should not be so hard to do.

It is very important to read the Bible more daily. We may soon be asked questions about our faith in GOD and why this or that. Our answers to those questions must be true and trustworthy because some people's future lives may depend on them. We all must be aware that if people around us can see our faith in GOD when they are in deep trouble, they will seek out a *real* Christian for advice. I think it is a grand thing for Christians to be prepared and able to give good answers to people like that.

Praying to, and praising GOD are ways of gaining Spiritual strength in our own lives and can give us the ability to pass it on to others. If we can just get past the temptations coming to us daily and maintain our prayer life, we will surely be stronger in GOD's service.

BOTTOM LINE: We would surely be wise to think on these things as we see perilous times approaching.

Your Notes & Scriptures:

58 – THE SEE-SAW OF LIFE

We should just praise the Lord for the present time and for the things happening around the world.

Consider the *SEE-SAW* of life. Christians are on one end, and the world is on the other end. When the *NEWS AND WORLD EVENTS* get so bad that it causes us to get depressed, we should remember that the bad news makes the world *heavier* so that when the world's end goes down, the Christians' end goes up, closer to GOD.

That should be enough to make us rejoice and be glad. I don't know about you, but I can hardly wait until we are taken out of this world. I can't think of any reason that I should ask GOD to wait any longer. Although there many things that I still should do, I am not going to worry about it one second. I believe the Bible tells us to be ready to let go of all things between us and the world.

When Christians *really* serve GOD, the allure of the things of the world gets less and less important to us and we are more ready for Jesus to come and call us out of here.

Although I am not a preacher or a judge, there seems to be lots of people who think they are saved and are trying to serve GOD the best they can. Think about what the Bible says; that if a person does not have the Holy Spirit, they are none of His.

Another question is, can a person receive forgiveness of sin, eternal life, and the indwelling of the Holy Spirit and not know it? Since all of GOD's work is of a spiritual nature, we do not have the power or knowledge to serve GOD without the help of His Spirit, which means a person may do the exact same things as Christians do and act the same way as others, but all of that is not worth the leg off of one grub-worm. One statement made in the Bible is, *"except the Lord builds the house, they labor in vain that build it"*. Human WORKS do not earn eternal life. A person must receive it as a *free gift* from GOD by trusting in Jesus Christ. Our works are another matter completely.

When I see a large gathering at some stadium or meeting place, I often wonder, if the Lord should come at that moment, how many would be left behind. I really wonder if enough people would be called out to the Lord for others to miss them. Some people believe if the Lord should come on Sunday morning during the church service, many services would go right on without any interruption. As sad as that sounds, it may very well be true.

BOTTOM LINE: We have no more time to play around with our service to the Lord.

Your Notes & Scriptures:……………………………………………….

59 – GOD'S DECREE

GOD does not demand control of this country or any other that I know of. Since GOD created all things, He actually owns it all anyway. He only steps in when it has to do with His plan, which He made before He created anything. GOD has made a decree that mankind will rule over the Earth. That means the animals, the fish of the sea, and everything that we have the power to control. GOD takes care of the things we cannot control such as the weather, storms on land, storms at sea and so on.

GOD does not demand control of our lives even after we have been saved. GOD wants us to obey Him because we love Him for forgiving our sins and giving us eternal life in His Kingdom. GOD also extends His watch care over us every day. After learning about what awaits the unsaved at the final Judgment, I dread to think about the people I know that are not saved. I believe we will be there at the final Judgment of the lost, and will see the ones that we had a chance to witness to, and did not. I don't know how that will work out, but I don't think it will be very good to see.

GOD wants to be the director of all of His churches. He wants to have a pastor who will be guided by the Holy Spirit in everything, and a staff that will follow the Pastor's leadership in all the workings of the Church. If the Pastor of any church gets out of line, or rebels against GOD, I believe that GOD is well able to take care of the problem.

I believe GOD wants to be the problem solver of our families and the one we call on when things get out of hand around the house. We can see from the past how important family life is. Although any family member can go astray, it is always better to have GOD to call upon. GOD is not going to make our lives a bed of roses, but He can always work things out for the best of everyone concerned. Sometimes we may wonder why some families have a lot more troubles than others. I don't have an answer for that, but I know that GOD does, and we can be sure that all things will be balanced out in the end.

BOTTOM LINE: Give GOD Control.

Your Notes & Scriptures:

60 – SPIRITUAL HAZE

A spiritual *haze* called SIN has been around the whole Earth since Adam and Eve sinned. It keeps the lost people blinded to the truth about Heaven and the only way to get there.

When a person is really BORN AGAIN, GOD places a light, called the Holy Spirit, in that person's soul and leaves them on the Earth to be a light to the lost. The person receiving the light also receives the power to witness to, and open the door of salvation and eternal life for any person who will believe the Gospel message and receive the gift of eternal life from GOD by accepting Jesus Christ as their personal Savior.

When true Christians come together to worship and praise GOD, it is like a great BEACON shining through the haze. The church building is not the Church. The people who have been saved are the Church and when they all come together, it's like they are all holding up a torch. Although some Christians may let their lights grow dim, they are still Christians and often have their lights brightened up when they hear the Gospel message preached.

The human body was not constructed to lounge around and do nothing. As the saying goes, *if you don't use it you lose it*. That must mean all the bodies moving parts. When Christians are serving the Lord by using the talents GOD gives them, they always feel better and more satisfied. When a Christian gets too old to serve physically, they can greet people, smile, make phone calls, tell someone a joke, or be willing to listen when someone just wants to talk. I think that when GOD does not have anything else for a Christian to do on this Earth, He will call them home to Heaven.

Although Christians in America are not yet persecuted like they are in other countries, the time seems to be near at hand when there will be some bad times coming for the true churches. I believe that *now* would be a good time to grow stronger in our faith before the real trouble gets here. If someone should point a gun at me and ask me to deny Jesus Christ, I want to have the faith to refuse, and stand firm in my belief. I believe one thing we can do is spend more time with other Christians and strengthen one another in our daily lives. We can also talk about our experiences and things we read about in the Bible. We can talk about GOD and speculate about our future in Heaven.

BOTTOM LINE: The strength we need to stand comes only from GOD and is available 24/7. That is the promise GOD has made to us who trust Him. All we have to do is accept it.

Your Notes & Scriptures:

61 – THE CHURCH'S DECLINE

According to some of the most learned, well read Christian men, the worst thing that could happen to our churches, started in the 50s and grew in the 60s and 70s. Some of the churches began to believe that the Bible only *contained* the Word of GOD, but was not all GOD's Word through and through. That great error has caused the decline of the pure Gospel in many of the *best* churches.

Now, many Christians, *good people*, have let their *lights* grow dim in their families and neighborhoods. It is harder now to find a *real* dedicated Christian that will let their light shine so bright that people around them know for sure that they are trust worthy and can be trusted to keep the secret things told to them. That is part of the result of diluting the Bible and the Gospel message.

Rebellion against parents and the law began in the 50s, when parents got so busy maintaining their *better* life style that they did not have much time for the kids. Not all people were that way then, but enough were to start a decline in raising children right and obeying GOD and the law.

I remember the time when most people did not lock their cars when they parked, but now we must lock our cars even in the church parking lot. We have sure come a long way. When I was growing up, my dad did not hesitate to take me and my brothers and sisters to the *woodshed* for an attitude adjustment. Instead of reporting him to the law, I respected him for his rules in our family.

The perilous times in the last days, spoken of by Jesus Himself, seem to be closing in on us. I think we may be living in the time when our lifestyle in our free country is soon to change for the worst. I don't mean to sound like a doomsday prophet, but there is just too much bad news coming to us to believe anything else. I don't see how some people can believe the way they do these days.

One of my friends was keeping his granddaughter and she did something to cause them to *ground* her. She secretly called the law and said that she was being abused. When the police came and told the grandparents about the call, the woman of the house said, I don't know of any abuse here, but when you leave, there will be. The policeman said, "I don't see any abuse here," and he left. So you see, there is still a little light left in this world.

BOTTOM LINE: Christian brothers and sisters: We have to decide now if we will stand firm in our faith when the time comes.

Your Notes & Scriptures:

62 – HONORING GOD

How can we honor GOD, with our lives and our daily living? When Jesus Christ was here on Earth, His greatest desire was for His followers believe in Him to the point of obeying and following Him daily. That desire has not changed. Jesus has not changed.

Jesus said that all power in Heaven and Earth was given to Him. Jesus has the power to supply our every need. If we need food, He is able to supply it. If we need money, He is able to supply it.

Jesus will entrust to us all the money and *stuff* that we are able to be responsible for. I have always thought I could handle a great fortune and live for GOD every day. Bad news: If GOD gave me any more than I have, I would probably go romping around the world and living it up.

Another way to honor GOD is through prayer. GOD knows our every need before we ask Him, but prayer is the way GOD has provided for us to talk directly to Him without going through another person. I know that many times our prayer lives fall short. But GOD is patient with us and wants to hear our sincere prayers to Him. Sometimes we may not get what we ask for but somewhere down the road, GOD will let us know that we would have been worse off, had He granted it.

Another way we can honor GOD is to develop a *caring* attitude. We should especially care for our Christian brothers and sisters. As Christians, we draw strength from each other when we enjoy fellowship together. We learn of each other's trials and troubles so that we can pray for one another. I don't know *exactly* what Heaven will be like, but I know some of the people who will be there. PRAISE GOD!

We would probably be better off if we just give GOD as much honor as we sometimes give to the sports figures and movie stars. At least that is a place to start. We can make our dedication and honor to GOD grow as time goes on. Reading our Bibles, attending church on a regular basis, praying daily, and sharing the Gospel message, are some of the things we can do as Christians. Our GOD is higher and in control of the highest Heaven. He *made* it. That means He is in control of everything else, including us, because He made all things.

BOTTOM LINE: Let's all start believing it.

Your Notes & Scriptures:

63 – MY PLAN VERSES GOD'S PLAN

"Dear GOD; I have a plan of how I want to serve you, and when I get it started I want you to bless it. I know it is a good one because I really spent some time working it out to fit in with my busy schedule."

Does that sound familiar? I'm afraid it fits many of us who are in the upper class in knowledge and wisdom; I wish. In the real world, most of us don't have the knowledge and wisdom to pour water out of a boot with directions on the toe and a faucet in the heel. *I mean that as it pertains to the spiritual world.* GOD has warned us that His wisdom and ways are higher than ours above the highest Heaven. GOD's knowledge and wisdom compared to us would be like us compared to ameba or germs. Serving GOD may not be easy all the time, but it is the best way to go, and the retirement plan is out of this world.

What does GOD really want from us when we are born again into His kingdom? When a little baby in born into a family, what does the family expect from the baby? The baby is usually lots of trouble. Only a mother has the patience to tend to him. By the time the baby is weaned the training starts and continues for a life time. They usually start to school at six years of age, and from there it is constant rebellion and correction. The child must be trained to be a responsible adult and to serve GOD when it becomes an adult. It has been said that if a parent wants their children to be *bad*, they just do nothing. By the nature all humans received from Adam after the fall, being bad is automatic. If children do not receive proper training at home, they will receive it in a dark alley from their peers. We are seeing a whole generation of them now and we can surely see the results from Washington DC outward in all directions.

What should we do? I have been told that if a child has not been trained at home by the age of ten years old, it will be doubly hard to get them to listen to authority. That seems to be the age that they think they know everything.

Here is a suggestion. Only GOD has the power to change a person on the inside. So, it makes good sense to obey GOD ourselves and pray that He will take care of and train the kids. I heard of one pastor of a church who was worried about his kids going to college. GOD told him plain, *"you do your preaching, and I will send the kids to College."*

BOTTOM LINE: We *must* give GOD control of our minds, worries, and fears.

Your Notes & Scriptures:

64 – REAL FAITH

Happy is a person who has real faith in the GOD of Heaven and Earth. That faith will let us have faith during our daily lives as well. We will find that we can enjoy our kids and grandkids without fear of doing the wrong thing before them, and casting a bad example. We can have confidence before our neighbors, our friends, and co-workers. Most of all, it is a grand feeling just to be in right tune with the Lord.

Sometimes we get the feeling of being unworthy of GOD's blessings. I have learned a couple of things through the years; one is that when a person is born again, GOD the Holy Spirit cleans out his soul and moves in and puts a *seal* around the soul so it can never again be touched by the evil forces. When GOD looks at us He sees the Holy Spirit instead of us, and will not charge anything against us. Although we are disciplined for the sin we commit while we are on this Earth, Jesus stands between us and GOD's judgment so that we can grow by the *woodshed* experience and grow closer to GOD.

When the Rapture comes, we will be caught up in the air to meet Jesus. We will be having great joy while the seven years Tribulation Period is going on. We don't really know all about how that will be, but we will be in the presence of Jesus, and the Bible says that we will be like Him. When I think about that, I think we will not care about what happened on this Earth during our lifetimes.

Make every move productive, every word count, and every thought meaningful. Think about GOD and the tender mercy He extends to us even when we sin against

Him. I believe GOD actually loves us more than anyone on this Earth does. As a matter of fact, if He didn't, none of us could survive. GOD is real, Heaven is real, and all the blessings that humans can receive are real.

How long will it be before Jesus calls His Church up to meet Him in the air? I don't know. I don't think anyone on this Earth knows, or anyone in Heaven either, except GOD the Father. With that thought in mind, what should we be doing? I am going to try to serve the Lord the best I can and live this life as a Christian light in this world.

BOTTOM LINE: It makes us feel good to think about Heaven and all its beauty. If we keep that in mind, I think our lives will go a little smoother.

Your Notes & Scriptures:

65 – RECEIVING RIGHTEOUSNESS

Christians cannot achieve righteousness by the good deeds and thoughts done in this life. Our GOD is so pure and holy that humans cannot see His face and live. Also, the violence that has come into the world has come slowly over the years so that even Christians are almost immune to the effect it has on our spirits. GOD is our only hope to help us keep our lights shining while we still live on this Earth.

If the Christian light goes out on this Earth, lost people will have nothing to see or turn to for hope of eternal life. Evil forces are working 24/7 to put out all evidence of Heaven and eternal life. We can see all this at work all over our country. If our best leaders are corrupt, how can we survive as a nation?

I should stop and say that not all the leaders in our country are corrupt. There are still Christian men and women who are in leadership positions in this country, but they are finding it harder and harder to maintain good and honest service in their workplace. It seems that just about the whole country has gone after *fun and games* and almost given up everything else.

Many Christians believe and are sure that the Church will soon be taken out of this world. The events happening around the world seem to point in that direction. It is hard for us to realize all that will take place when that happens. Christians driving cars will be taken up and the cars will crash. Other things Christians will be doing will be left instantly and whatever happens there will happen.

When the Church is taken up, the evil forces will try to take control of the whole Earth. Although GOD will allow them to fulfill His will for the end time, they will never be in complete control. Many people will be saved during that period of time. As long as we can remember that GOD is always in control of events happening on the Earth, then we can have more confidence when we pray and depend on GOD for our safety and future in Heaven.

Talking about all these things tends to boggle our minds, but we need to remember that these events are real and are sure to come to pass. One thing we need to remember is that there are a lot of *good* people around us that are not saved. Most lost people don't know they are lost. They can only know when they are told. That is the job of GOD's children.

BOTTOM LINE: When Jesus comes back I hope I don't have to look into the face of my neighbor who is in a lost condition, when I could have told him before these final events happen.

Your Notes & Scriptures:

66 – SODOM AND GOMORRAH

The sins of Sodom and Gomorrah had spread up to Heaven. That meant that there were no *greater* sins that they could do to make themselves worse. GOD saw that they would continue to bring children into the world only to live and die and be condemned to eternal death. As an act of *mercy*, GOD sent His angels to utterly destroy both cities and the surrounding villages where that kind of life style was practiced.

Today, in some parts of the world, that same type of lifestyle is carried on. There is one difference that exists today that did not exist back then. When Jesus came to Earth and finished His ministry and then died on the Cross, He carried the fountain of blood He shed for all mankind and placed it before GOD the Father, creating a *Stay of Execution* for mankind until the Church is completed.

That does not mean that GOD opened the door for *free* sin for the world. It means that He has committed all judgment to GOD the Son, Jesus, who is now judging the hearts of those who call on His name for forgiveness of sin and eternal life. People should realize that GOD is not going to allow anyone to come before Him and speculate about accepting Jesus or not. If a person is not sincere about asking, you just as well forget it.

The Great GOD is not going to play games with us; not the lost or the saved. Sin is sin and to be sure GOD does know the difference between a sincere heart and a false one. GOD's Law is still very much in effect. If we break GOD's law and don't get forgiveness, whether we are saved or lost, we will pay the price. By the way, the price is *very* high.

It seems that no matter how hard America tries to throw GOD out of the country, He just will not go. The reason I know that is because He is still blessing His Children. He is still answering prayers and caring for the needs of His sons and daughters. I think when GOD does get ready to leave He will take all His saints with Him. Personally, when GOD decides to go and take us with Him, I don't care what they do with this country. I am going to be in another *country* much better than this one.

BOTTOM LINE: Come go with us. You will like *that* change.

Your Notes & Scriptures:

67 – TEST ON PLANT LIFE

A test was run on two pot-plants in a laboratory. The two identical plants were set on a shelf and one had wires from a lie detector connected to its leaves and stems. A policeman in uniform came in and drew his gun and shot the plant that was not hooked up several times. The other plant showed a violent reaction as the needles moved back and four across the screen. Other people came in and went out several times and the plant did not move. The policeman came through the door and the plant once again showed a violent reaction. Then the policeman went out and changed from his uniform into regular clothes and once again came through the door. Once again the plant showed a violent reaction. What does all this have to do with anything?

Every physical thing that was created is dead! All of the bodies created for every creature, including humans had no life at all until GOD placed a measure of His Spirit into that body. The function of that Spirit is to keep that body alive and working right. According to the Bible, when that spirit leaves the body, the body dies and goes back to dust. Although mankind has the same spirit tending his body, there is a difference between mankind and animals. GOD breathed into Adam's nostrils and he became a living soul. That means that mankind has the ability to walk and talk with GOD Himself.

The sum of this is that neither angels, humans, animals, birds, fish, trees, plants, nor grass have any life at all aside from the spirit of life that GOD has placed in each living thing on this Earth. I guess that means that GOD owns all the life on Earth. And more than that, He can recall it any time He wants without being bad or unjust or unfair. I think this also means that everything we have actually belongs to GOD and He simply lends it to us while we are on this Earth. For example, Peter did not walk on that water toward Jesus by his own power. Jesus was the one holding him up. When peter started to sink, he didn't try to pray *through*. He cried out, "Lord save me!" and we all know Jesus did.

BOTTOM LINE: I think we had better give up all this power we *think* we have and surrender to GOD's will for our lives.

Your Notes & Scriptures:

68 – CHRISTIAN JOY

A Christian's Joy is found only in Righteousness. But alas, we have none of ourselves. Think of one of the rare times when you were completely in the Spirit and experiencing the Joy that comes only from GOD himself. We would like to stay that way all the time, however, our daily lives and activities keeps us from doing so. We still have a daily battle to fight with the forces of evil that would destroy us in a second if GOD would allow. If GOD did allow us to live at such heights, we would be unreachable by anybody around us. Remember, our main purpose for being saved and left in this world is to show the light, which GOD gave us, to the world so some may be saved.

When GOD took away our sins He replaced them with His own righteousness. That is why we can be called Christians; we have Jesus' Spirit living inside our souls. That provides the power to lead anyone who will listen to Jesus Christ for forgiveness of sin and eternal life. All we furnish is the feet to go and the tongue to speak.

Remember, Jesus said, *"Whosoever comes to me I will in no wise cast out."* We all know that if GOD could change His mind and hold us responsible for all our sins, no one could survive. GOD does not want to condemn the world; He wants all people to be saved. I am sure GOD grieves over us when we fall away, even for a little while but I am so glad He is always willing to take us back when we repent and turn from our wicked ways. I think this all means that GOD would have us to show *His* righteousness to the world instead of our feeble attempt at being good.

The best way to do that is to study GOD's Word and find out just what is involved in showing His righteousness instead of ours. The more we try to be holy on our own, the harder the battle becomes. Many mature Christians will tell you that we cannot win the battle with Satan with our own power. We will lose every time. Also GOD said the battle was His anyway. I think it takes time to really learn that and it is a good lesson to learn.

BOTTOM LINE: When we finally learn that GOD wants to fight our battles with Satan we can began to live in the righteousness GOD has given us and know the joy GOD meant for us to have. Let's give it a try!

Your Notes & Scriptures:

69 – AT YOUR HOUSE

What would be happening at your house if Jesus had come for His Church 10 minutes ago? Would there be weeping and wailing and praying? Who would be left behind? I think sometimes we just cannot see it happening in our lifetime. The Bible says that one day people will say to Christians, *"You keep talking about Jesus' coming, so where is he? Everything is still going on as usual."* Actually some people are saying that now. Some are trying to rush it up by setting a time for it to happen.

Some people are trying to decipher codes out of the Bible and figure out the chain of events that GOD has set that only He knows about. After thinking about the end time events, I am not so sure that I need to know about all the details. As a matter of fact, I don't think I could handle that much knowledge because my mind is not big enough. I guess I had better leave that up to GOD and just fall in line with the other Christians.

As far as being *ready* for the Rapture is concerned, I think most of us will be just as ready tomorrow as we are today. The Bible says that when we least expect it, He will come. GOD has told us over and over that we don't know when He will come. We should always be ready. I think that I have finally learned that it is only by the grace of GOD that I will enter His kingdom.

When I figured that out, it took a big load off my mind. Now if Jesus calls us out of this world in a few minutes or next week or next month it is going to be a great time of reunion with all the saints. I get goose bumps every time I think about it, but I am not in a hurry to face the Judgment seat of Jesus Christ. I know it is coming to all Christians but I have not been a real good boy all the time. The best thing about that is Jesus knows all about that and if He is willing to save a *thing* like me, I am not going to worry about the future that I have no control over.

GOD has said that when His Word goes out it will not return unto Him void. I think that means it is our job to spread His Word around and let Him take care of the results. There seems to be several ways to do that, but the old-fashioned word of mouth has always been the best way.

BOTTOM LINE: Take the name of Jesus with you wherever you go.

Your Notes & Scriptures:

70 – WHAT YOU DO

"EVERY THING YOU BEGAN TO DO, DO IT WITH ALL YOUR MIGHT!" (! Cor. 10:31)

When I remembered that verse in the Bible, I took a little survey of myself about the things I do, both public and private, and found that often times I am off in *never land* while I am doing something I need to do. Other times I may count that chore as unimportant.

Then I remembered some things that I really counted as important and *worked* hard to do the job. When I did that, the job was so easy and sometimes *fun* to do. And, after it was done, there was a certain satisfaction in doing it. After pondering these things, I wonder just how much we lose in our daily lives by being lazy and half-hearted about our daily chores.

The Bible says that in the very beginning, GOD made Adam to *till* the Garden of Eden and not to lay around with his mouth open for GOD to fill it. I believe that means that our bodies are made to do work and remain active as long as possible. Those may be the best health benefits we can find.

This train of thought could be applied to all our *goings* in our lives, like reading the Bible, reading the paper, studying for our Sunday School lesson, paying attention during the Worship Service, *listening to our wives or husbands*, and the list goes on and on. I am going to try to take *Mister Laziness* by the nap of the neck and throw him as far as I can. I'll replace him with *"I can do it"* thinking and see how that makes a difference in my daily living. However, I don't want anyone to ask me about it because if it works out, it will be good. But if it does not, I don't want anyone to know it.

As you all know we put on our best manner and *face* when we go out among other people. I think it is better that way because enough rumors are already flying everywhere and we don't need to cause any more. We Christians should be the example for the world to see. If we can do things that will bring a smile of satisfaction on our face, I can tell you for sure the world will see it.

Remember, we are the only light the world has to see. We just can't afford to show misery and a *down in the mouth* attitude all the time. Doing so will cause many to turn away from GOD's gift of salvation and eternal life.

BOTTOM LINE: No matter how loud the old muscles squeak and bones crack, we need to move as much as possible.

Your Notes & Scriptures:

71 – TWO DOGS INSIDE

Someone once said that living the Christian life was like having two dogs inside of them that fight all the time; one white and one black. Someone asked him which one of the dogs win and he replied, *"The one I feed the most."* If that is true, and it may be, we might be wise to examine the food it takes to feed each one of them.

The original sin was caused by a High Angel's lust for power. Lucifer, *Satan,* saw the beauty GOD gave him when he was created, and decided he should be up as high as GOD and share His power and authority. Well, Satan was cast out and removed from his high position in Heaven. I am sure Satan went into a rage and decided to destroy everything GOD created.

Satan was there when GOD created Adam and Eve and knew their weaknesses. Being as evil and clever as he is, he came to Eve and appealed to her desire for knowledge, *or power*, and caused her to disobey GOD and eat the forbidden fruit. From there it has been a constant fight between good and evil. Satan wants to give all humans his lust for power and authority. That seems to come when a baby is born. As a child grows, its desire for power and authority grows with them.

When we do something great or even good, we want somebody to see it. It feels good to sit behind the wheel of a car and feel the power of a big engine. The temptation to *burn off* or spin out comes to almost every person, *males mostly.* Things that go with the lust for power are listed in the Bible titled *"the fruit of the flesh."* If the flesh is allowed to grow, it will soon become an uncontrollable monster and the Spirit will grow weaker and weaker.

Only GOD can pull a person out of the *sin trap* and wipe away all past sins and guarantee forgiveness for the rest of their life. That is GOD's promise to anyone who will trust His Son Jesus Christ for their salvation. GOD's free gift of salvation does not take away the old nature. The same desires are there but can be overcome by the power of the Holy Spirit. That is where the human mind becomes the neutral zone and makes the decisions to follow GOD and grow in grace, or return to the bad side.

Food for the Christian's spirit is Bible study, prayer, Christian fellowship, attending Church, worshiping GOD and serving GOD through His Church.

BOTTOM LINE: We can either serve GOD or the evil one. The choice is ours.

Your Notes & Scriptures:

72 – ROAD MAP TO HEAVEN

Many things have been spoken about the Bible. But among other things, the Bible is a road map. In the hands of a Christian it can show any person how to reach Heaven where everything is perfect. We cannot even imagine the beauty and peace in the place called Heaven, where GOD lives.

The first stop for that person is the Cross; *the death of Jesus for our sins*. There the person's sin will be exposed before GOD but *not* before people. God already knows all about the person anyway. It is necessary for that person to realize that sin cannot remain in GOD's presence and must be removed. When that person acknowledges their sin before GOD, then GOD removes all past sin from their souls. The Holy Spirit moves in and puts a seal around that soul so it can never be touched again by the evil one. Although the *old* nature, the desire to sin, remains, that person now has access to the power to overcome the temptations that come every day.

Now this new Christian has the knowledge to recognize temptations when they come and GOD is always willing to help His new child overcome them. Sometimes the new Christian does not take GOD's offer to overcome temptation and they fall back into their old sins. It is amazing, but GOD is always willing to take that person back when they admit their sin and ask for forgiveness. When that happens and the person is restored back to fellowship with GOD, they begin again to learn about their new position in GOD's Kingdom.

That may be the best promise GOD has made to humans, that is, to offer forgiveness for sins for the rest of their lives. It is like Jesus said, that if a person does something to you and turns and asks for forgiveness, you must forgive them seventy times seven times in any day. That is not easy; in fact we could not do without GOD's help. But that is the type of person GOD wants us to be while we live on this Earth.

The second stop for the new Christian is the church. There the new Christian is baptized and brought into the fellowship of the church and all its members. There, the new Christian begins to learn about different services Christians do in and around the church. The opportunities are almost unlimited and open where a person can serve. After the new Christian matures, they may serve as a Deacon, or Teacher, or a Witness to the lost, or visit the sick in the hospital or those shut-in at home, or a host of other things that need to be done in and for the church.

BOTTOM LINE: Come and find out the *real* joy of being a Christian.

Your Notes & Scriptures:

73 – THE BODY AND SOUL

The soul, *or spirit,* of mankind is seen from Heaven. The bodies of mankind are seen from Earth. The actions, *or works,* of mankind are always open and visible to GOD at all times and places. Not only does GOD see our *goings,* He also knows the reasons and intent of our hearts. This knowledge leaves us with two different *thoughts* to consider, concerning our Spiritual condition in this life and after death.

The sins people commit on this Earth feed directly into their souls. That means that from the first sin to the present time, all sins committed by that person show in Heaven before GOD, meaning all unsaved people. There is no known way for anyone to remove those sins from their own souls. Many people try by doing good deeds or works. The problem is that the Bible says that all our *goodness* is the same as filthy rags in GOD's sight. Now, I think that would make Him sick.

The truth is, our good deeds are not acceptable in His sight. Of course, that demands further explanation. We are in a fallen state (the state before Adam fell from GOD's grace) and we are unable to restore ourselves into GOD's grace. Only GOD is able to go into a person's soul and remove the sins and make that person pure before Him.

When a person realizes they are lost in sin and unable to save themselves, they can call upon the name of Jesus Christ, confess that they are a sinner, and ask for forgiveness. GOD is so tender hearted He will not turn that person away no matter what condition they may be in. Then GOD will come into that person's heart, take out all the past sins and restore fellowship with them. Then He will move into the soul and put a seal around it so it cannot be touched ever again by the evil forces. After that, the new Christian becomes baptized into the local church and begins training for GOD's service and learning of the real joy of being a Christian.

The actions and lifestyle that Christians live on this Earth are all that the lost people have to see and is the *light* Jesus told us to let shine before world. Make no mistake; people do see what Christians do. When you get up and go to church on Sunday morning, someone is going to see. You may not know it, but you will be surprised just how many that is.

BOTTOM LINE: Serve GOD with gladness of heart.

Your Notes & Scriptures:

74 – THE SUBSTANCE OF HOPE

"FAITH IS THE SUBSTANCE OF THINGS HOPED FOR, THE EVIDENCE OF THINGS NOT SEEN." Heb. 11:1.

The explanation of this scripture from the Earthly view is, **Hope**, *STAGE ONE*. All the people in the world have a *built-in* HOPE to go to some type of Heaven that was instilled in mankind when GOD breathed the breath of life into Adam's nostrils. Even though Adam fell from GOD's grace, the desire to be with GOD was not lost. Many people have different gods and all hope their god can help them and take them to Heaven when they die.

The *SECOND STAGE* is **Faith**. On Earth humans have a problem with faith because they usually only have faith in things of the world, like riding in a car down the highway at 70 miles per hour and feeling safe or sitting in a chair and having the faith that it will not break and fall.

The *THIRD STAGE* is **Substance**. Suppose I want, or *hope* to build a beautiful chair for my house. Hope gives me the initiative to go get a plan with dimensions and instructions to build a chair. Faith makes me believe that I can do it. So, I gather up the lumber, nails, screws, and paint to finish my chair. Now the chair is finished and the paint is dry and I am looking at the *substance* of my work.

In the spiritual realm all we have from birth is *hope*. GOD must provide the spiritual faith and instill it into our hearts before we can accept Jesus Christ as our personal Savior. The Bible says that faith comes by *hearing* and hearing comes by the Word of GOD, *the Bible*. After enough faith comes into a person's heart to accept Jesus

Christ and be Born Again, that faith begins to grow as the person studies and learns from the Bible.

Although our faith is called substance, the final end of our faith is when GOD comes and takes His saints out of this world via the Rapture. That is when we will see the final substance of our salvation.

BOTTOM LINE: I asked three mature Ministers of the Faith, from different locations, to give their interpretations and comments on this subject. I was amazed that their answers were almost identical.

Your Notes & Scriptures:

75 – GOD CAME

GOD THE SON CAME TO EARTH. When GOD saw it was time to come to Earth, as GOD the Son, to redeem mankind from the penalty of SIN, He came and was born to a teenage virgin girl named Mary. Joseph, her husband-to-be, was instructed to name the child Jesus, for He would save His people from their sins. This meant that Jesus, (His Earthly name) Christ, (His Heavenly name), could hold our hands, and hold GOD's hand at the same time, making a perfect road to Heaven for us. Jesus made it very clear that the only way to Heaven was through Him. With that in mind, it makes good sense to go to the Holy Bible for the details on coming to Jesus for forgiveness of sin and Christian living while we live on this Earth.

Once a year we set time aside to celebrate Jesus' birth. We call it Christmas because it is a perfect time to tell the story. Notice the word *Christmas* has the name Christ in it. I don't know about you, but in my house, the word Christmas is going to stay as long as I do. I believe exchanging gifts creates a happy time, and since many angels were singing and rejoicing before the shepherds, I believe GOD would have us to do the same when we celebrate Jesus' birth. I know we have gone overboard with our gift giving, but the celebration is the same. I believe we should always remember where our salvation and spiritual joy comes from.

In this country we have many different Christian denominations, but most of them celebrate Christmas the same way. That could mean that many of them are similar in worship of GOD and service to Him. It would be great if we could all come closer to GOD because of that.

GOD's great adversary, the evil one, will use everything in his power to destroy GOD's work and bring grief to GOD and His children. We should always be aware that the evil that comes on us is not brought by GOD. Although we are disciplined by GOD, He does it like a Father would correct his precious child. The evil one is more clever and subtle than any human on this Earth. We should never think we can take a little taste of his goodies, and let it go at that. He will not let us get by with that. One little taste will lead to two more and so on until we are completely destroyed. The battle between GOD and the evil one seems to take place in our minds. If we turn away from GOD, then there is no place to go except to fall prey to the evil one. The evil one will make a person think they are serving GOD and doing good but the Bible says we should *try* (test) the spirits to see if they are good or evil.

BOTTOM LINE, Ask GOD about it.

Your Notes & Scriptures:

76 – THE SEVENTH CHURCH

Are our churches growing colder as time goes on? We are seeing a decline in the attendance to the churches where the true Gospel is preached. This would be in line with the 7th Church, named Laodicea, and recorded by the Apostle John in the Bible book of The Revelation. In that record the Laodicea Church was neither cold nor hot. Jesus said, *"Because you are neither cold nor hot, but are Luke warm, I will spew you out of my mouth,"* which means *"I, GOD, will shut you down so you will have to close the doors."* We can take a sip of Luke warm coffee to see what Jesus was talking about. It tastes terrible!

The attack on Christianity can be seen all across our country and around the world. It seems the evil forces are working hard to take GOD out of our country and the Spirit out of our churches. Can this be the beginning of the end of time as we know it? If we follow the news about our country and most of the foreign countries, we will see clearly how the events recorded in the Bible book of The Revelation are taking shape around the world. Jesus said to His followers, *"When you see these things coming to pass, look up for your redemption draws near."* Still, we would be wise to not be shaken in mind because of all this. I believe GOD still has a lot of things for us to do while His plan is being carried out.

I hope everyone in our town is saved and ready for the Rapture to take place, but I cannot see evidence of that. There are too many people around here who totally disregard the teachings of the Bible. Many think they are good enough to go to Heaven, others say they have plenty of time, others say, I'll think about that and get back with you later. All of that will *not* get anyone into Heaven. GOD the Son, Jesus, gave up His own life so that we would not have to give up ours. Jesus also said that anyone trying to get into Heaven except through Him was a thief and a robber. I don't think GOD can say it any plainer than that. I have heard it said that anyone who comes to realize they are a sinner and cannot save themselves, and asks GOD three times in secret, GOD will answer and tell them what to do. I can't verify that but that's what I heard.

BOTTOM LINE: Jesus died on the cross, was buried, and arose the third day to show that He is in charge of life and death. When people accept Jesus as their Savior, their life and death is secure in His hands.

Your Notes & Scriptures:

WILLIE HOLT

77 – CHRISTIAN DUTY

I believe a Christian's Civil Duty should begin at home. If a home looks like a junk yard, it is like a great *sore* on the neighborhood. It seems to paint a picture of what the people who live there are really like. Not many of the neighbors would care to visit them. Keeping the home and yard cleaned up should be a top priority for any family especially if the family members are Christians.

Christians should know something about the town and county leaders who we vote for to fill the positions of leadership in the community. We don't have to have a complete history on them, but we don't need to vote *blind* when election time comes around. Voting without any knowledge of the candidates may be part of the reason our country is in trouble today. Although we don't have the power or authority to demand that all our leaders are Christians, it would be great if most of them were. The only actual power we have is prayer. If we would make it a habit to pray before we vote or do any service to the community, I believe we would see a big difference in the place where we live.

The next place where we should be concerned is our State Government. Although we vote for a small portion of the leadership there, we can do our best to know a little about who we vote for. The leaders there have a great responsibility to tend to schools, highways, taxes, jobs, veterans, and senior citizens, just to name a few. I wonder if it would be possible to have a county-wide meeting to hear a little about the people we vote for.

The next and greatest responsibility we have is the Government leaders in Washington D.C. I think most Christian people have already decided who to vote for there, but there may be other things to think about. We believe and are sure that GOD's plan for the end time is beginning to unfold before our eyes. Of course no one knows the details of that but some of the *signs* are already happening, which are spoken of in the Bible book of The Revelation. As Christians I believe we will be able to stand firm when the time comes because we should all stay prayed up and as close to GOD as possible.

BOTTOM LINE: Christians; don't be dismayed at what has happened in America, GOD is in charge and I think he can handle it. Praise His Name!

Your Notes & Scriptures:

78 – DOING THINGS MY WAY

I often try to do things my way, and in a hurry. When I do, they usually don't go very well. After close examination, I find it to be part of the old nature we received at birth. And, it can be traced all the way back to Adam, who rebelled against GOD and sinned by eating the forbidden fruit. GOD had warned him about it when Adam was created. Gaining the knowledge of good and evil, and being a human, he could never resist the temptations of the Devil.

Not much has changed today, we still want to do things our way, and we are still in human flesh and as weak as Adam was. When a person is saved, GOD does not remove the old nature, but leaves it for us to grow by. Without trials, we would remain children spiritually, the same as if we never learned anything physically. In that case we would be small children the rest of our lives.

If parents tell their children not to do something, the curiosity gets the best of them, and they will do it anyway. Example: One time when we lived on the farm we had several animals; horses, mules and cows with their calves. My older sister and I were just kids and when Mom and Dad had to go down the road to visit some neighbors, they told us, *"Don't you kids try to ride those calves."* We had never thought of riding them, but as soon as they said that, we had to try it. My older sister put me on one of the calves and tied my legs underneath with wire. Disaster struck in a hurry when the calf ran through the fence and drug me around until my legs came loose.

We learned a lesson that day; that Mom and Dad might know more than we did. Although we learned that lesson the hard way we soon forgot it and got into other things just as bad. Things like this simply show what GOD has to put up with 24/7 with His children. That is why He had to extend His love and forgiveness for the rest of our lives.

BOTTOM LINE: Thank and praise GOD every day. AMEN!

Your Notes & Scriptures:

79 – GOOD VERSES EVIL

GOOD versus EVIL. Who is good? Who is evil? What happened to us?

Note: This Column is written in plain talk, for the purpose of gaining more knowledge about this subject and applying the results to our daily lives. With that in mind, read this under those guidelines.

Jesus Christ would not allow His followers to call Him good. He said, *"Why do you call me good? There is only one good, that is, GOD."* I believe the reason He said that was, He still had a human body, and the human body is very limited in the ability to sustain itself. That means that anyone or anything that has some kind of limitation is not perfect, and therefore not totally *good*.

Now if that is true, then even angels live by GOD's power and are not self sufficient in and of themselves. That would be the *state* of Satan when he was created. All we know about Satan is that he was not satisfied with his life, and wanted to rise up to GOD's Throne and have the same power GOD has.

Since that was not possible Satan was cast down. We don't know what all that means, however I believe if Satan had been left beside GOD's Throne, he would have tried to overthrow GOD and take over everything himself. As far as we know, that was the beginning of evil. It appears that Satan went into a rage after he was cast down and vowed to destroy everything GOD made and all He did.

Adam and Eve were the first humans created on the Earth and did not know about good and evil. They were completely innocent before GOD and could walk with Him on the Earth. Since they were given a free will to make choices on their own, GOD knew they would have to be tested to see if they would obey His rules and live in a perfect paradise forever. GOD only asked them to do one thing for Him, and that was to not eat from the *Tree of Knowledge of Good and Evil.* He warned them that if they did, they would lose everything including their lives.

We all know the story how Satan tempted them and they did eat from the forbidden tree. Several things happened when they ate the fruit. First they lost their innocence, second they were separated from GOD, *(that is called Spiritual Death),* third, no human lived to be one thousand years old, *(one of GOD'S **days**).* That was the physical death GOD warned them about.

Since all humans descended from Adam, we have all inherited his sinful nature and are all sinners before GOD. We are by nature members of the evil side. No matter how good we try to be, we have no power to change our nature. Since GOD's plan is to reclaim humankind, and since He is the one who has the power to change us, we only have to ask for His cleaning.

BOTTOM LINE: If GOD doesn't do it, it won't be done.

Your Notes & Scriptures:

80 – KNOWLEDGE

KNOWLEDGE: How important is it? Why must we have it?

There was once a certain man who walked down the aisle and prayed the sinner's prayer and went to work in the church doing a number of things that needed to be done. He taught Sunday school lessons for over 50 years. One time he was listening to a preacher in a revival and discovered that he was not saved. The Holy Spirit revealed it to him at that time. When he prayed that prayer at a young age, he did not understand why he needed to be saved.

The job of the Holy Spirit on this Earth is to take the Gospel when it is preached and convince a person that they are lost and cannot save their own souls. They *must* believe that Jesus died on the cross to pay for their sins, and He is the only one who can clean the soul of all past sins. Unless a person is made to understand that, they will not receive salvation. It seems that whatever a person receives when they pray for salvation is what they will grow in. The Devil must be delighted when people don't understand about asking for salvation.

A person could not go up to a farmer and say, *"I am going to work for you today. I am going to go over there and cut those weeds behind the barn."* The farmer then would say, *"I don't need those weeds cut right now. I want you to go and plow up that field for planting time."* Then they would say, *"I don't want to plow today, I want to cut those weeds."* What do you think that farmer would say to that?

How often do we run out somewhere and try to work for GOD where He does not send us. You see, understanding what GOD wants us to do for Him comes by studying His Word and praying for guidance each day. GOD has the right to guide His children each day, and He will, if we will only trust Him.

I believe GOD *longs* to give us more understanding of Himself and His Word when we are able to be still and receive it. One of our worst problems is being too busy to listen. I have to admit that I want to stay in my comfort zone more and more these days. Maybe I am a *tiny* bit lazy, but I love for GOD to speak to me.

BOTTOM LINE: Let us pray for those people who are not saved, but think they are.

Your Notes & Scriptures:

81 – CHRISTIAN UNDERSTANDING

Why don't we understand the Bible better when we read it every day….almost?

I'm afraid we often times read the Bible as a book rather than the Word of the living personal GOD. If we don't have the Holy Spirit as a guide when reading it, we are just reading a book. I have heard many people say that they have read a certain scripture a hundred times, yet one day they read it and it comes alive and gives a message from GOD.

I remember a time in my life that I loved reading the Bible. It was so interesting and I got a certain joy from reading it but now I seem to struggle with it more and more. I think it may be caused by having so much *stuff* going on and so many activities to claim my attention. I thought that when I retired that I would have lots of time to do things, but I seem to be busy all the time. And what makes it worse; most of the things I do, I am doing for *myself*. I thank GOD for the best church in the world to go to and hear the *real* Gospel preached and fellowship with *real* Christians on Sunday morning. I seem to come away with a renewed Spirit each time I go.

Another drawback to sitting down and reading the Bible is, I am often full of the day's activities and have to struggle to get everything cleared out to really study it. Reading the Bible and *studying* are is two different things. I need to stop and ask myself what GOD is saying to me.

One good thing in Bible study is to have Bible study meetings with other Christians. It is so strange how one person can learn from another when they're in an informal meeting, often in someone's house. People tend to be more candid when in that type of meeting. Remember Jesus said, *"Where two or three are gathered together in my name, I am in their midst."* That type of meeting is a joy to be in.

Another great benefit from studying the Bible is, as we learn more and more about GOD's Word our troubles seem to be less and less, and often get smaller and smaller. GOD is not going to take away our troubles but He wants to help us with them. I believe GOD gets pleasure from helping one of His children through a trial.

BOTTOM LINE: Remember, if we do what GOD says, GOD does what He says.

Your Notes & Scriptures:

82 – MY OLD SELF AND MY NEW SELF

My old self wants everything in sight. It wants a wide easy road to travel on and lots of fun and games along the way. It wants to have a lot of riches and no responsibilities to go with them. It wants to be free to taste of everything this world has to offer. It wants to be naughty and for everyone to overlook it saying, *"Oh well, boys will be boys."*

It wants to have everything its own way. It wants everyone else to obey the law, but not be accused of anything bad itself. It wants to be bragged on and admired by everyone around close. It wants to be smart and clever and for everyone to know it. It wants to enjoy perfect health all its life and have no pain. It wants to be loved by everyone and only give it back when it wants to. In other words, this *old* man is rude, selfish, and rebellious against GOD, it hates authority and just about everything that is good. *I CAN'T BELIEVE I AM WRITING ALL THIS!*

My new *born again self* is just the opposite. GOD has come and cleaned up the old man and put His own love, righteous, caring, with His own Holy Spirit, inside the old man and made him a new creation. GOD has taken out the old heart of stone and put a *soft* heart in its place.

In addition, GOD has given the new man a complete new outlook on life. He has given new desires, new thoughts, and spirit. It is not like I thought it would be. I first thought GOD would take all of the fun out of my life and make me go around with a one hundred pound weight on my back. Instead, He has shown me what a real man should be, and what a joy it is when I act like one.

In order for me to grow in GOD's Holy Spirit, GOD has left the old man with me. Now, the old desires are still there. However, GOD has given me direct access to His own Thrown Room to pray and talk to Him about my troubles. He has also granted me the power to overcome the temptations of the Devil. The one thing we have to remember is this, GOD does *not* leave His power with us. GOD's power is always available to us but it is always under GOD's control. Because we still live in the *flesh* while we are on this Earth, we cannot be given the faith to throw mountains at our enemies.

BOTTOM LINE: The Christian life is not easy but more often than not, it is exciting.

Your Notes & Scriptures:

83 – ABOUT KING SOLOMON

Solomon was not a strong man like his father King David but He was the one chosen by GOD Himself to take David's place as King of Israel. When Solomon was crowned King he was overwhelmed with the responsibility of ruling over such a vast number of people. GOD appeared to him in a dream one night and asked him what he would wish for the most. Solomon told GOD that he was not able to rule over this great nation because he was young and inexperienced.

So Solomon asked GOD for wisdom to be a good King and rule over the people well. Solomon's request pleased GOD because he did not ask for riches or long life. GOD again spoke to Solomon and said, *"Because you did not ask for riches and long life, I am going to add those things to you, also, you will have more wisdom than any man has had before you or will have after you."*

King Solomon was given the task of building a temple where GOD would meet with His people, Israel. King David, Solomon's father had already gathered most of the materials to build this great structure. Solomon finished gathering the materials and the job began.

Solomon hired several thousand workers and many skilled masons, and wood and metal workers. After several years of work the temple was completed, Solomon dedicated the temple and all the utensils inside. The people came from everywhere to worship and see this beautiful sight.

The Nation of Israel was at peace in this time period and all the nations round about brought gifts of gold, silver, and precious stone in huge amounts. They also brought the most beautiful young women in their countries. As a result of this, Solomon became so wealthy that they stopped counting and just piled it up. Solomon also ended up with some three hundred wives and seven hundred live-in girlfriends. It has been said that he had forty thousand servants in his castle. Each one of the tribes of Israel supplied food for his household for one month out of the year.

Solomon built many lakes to water the fruit and nut trees he had planted. He did everything a man can do on this Earth, in other words he had it *all*. WELL, THAT WAS NOT ENOUGH TO SATISIFY HIM. When he stepped back and looked at all he had and did he had this to say. *"Vanity of vanities, all is vanity. Someone else is going to have all of this when I die and how do I know whether he will be wise or a fool. When I die, I will die just like the poorest person in my kingdom. When I die, I will not be remembered very long. What good is all I have done?"*

BOTTOM LINE: Let us use and enjoy what we have.

Your Notes & Scriptures:

84 – OUR RELATIONSHIP WITH GOD

HOW OFTEN DO WE TAKE OUR RELATIONSHIP WITH GOD FOR GRANTED?

I seem to go my own way, *in my mind* and forget about including GOD in my life and actions more often these days than in the past. Why is that? Am I growing colder spiritually? It seems that the more I try to be Holy and serve GOD each day, the more distractions seem to cross my path.

I think I need to hear the Gospel preached as often as I can. I have been told that my spirit needs food just as much as my body needs food to survive. Reading the Bible every day is another place to get spiritually fed, and cause my spirit to grow. Enjoying fellowship with other Christians is also food for my spirit. It seems to me that if we want to spend eternity with GOD, maybe we should learn more about our relationship with GOD, and what it means to be faithful to His instructions given to us in His Word.

Is GOD unreasonable? **NO**. I don't think GOD is unreasonable when He corrects His children. Human parents are not unreasonable when they correct their kids. So how much higher are GOD's ways than our ways and His thoughts than ours? GOD's law is perfect and no human is capable of keeping it perfectly. Jesus had to keep it for us. Otherwise no human could go to Heaven. Jesus gave His life on the cross to have the authority and power to save any person that would accept His gift of eternal life, by which all past sins of that person are wiped away and their souls are pure and clean before GOD.

The Bible says when a person accepts GOD's gift of eternal life even the angels in Heaven rejoice over it. Now, if all of Heaven is made to rejoice over one sinner who comes to Christ for salvation, shouldn't we be trying to get everyone to accept this gift from GOD?

I have been hearing from several reliable sources that we are surely living in the last days before Christ comes again to take His Church out of this world. It could be a long time before then, but we can't deny that world events are fulfilling the Bible prophecies more and more. Christians should look up because, like Jesus said, our redemption is near. The Rapture is the grandest hope and dream of every Christian today.

BOTTOM LINE: Let's don't fool around and be caught unaware and be embarrassed before all the saints and angels of Heaven.

Your Notes & Scriptures:

85 – THE *HEART* CHRISTIAN VERSES THE *MIND* CHRISTIAN

What is the difference between the *Heart* Christian and the *Mind* Christian?

The *Heart* Christian worships GOD from the Heart, while the *Mind* Christian worships GOD from the Mind. Both go to church, both attend most of the services of the church, both work in the church, both often teach Sunday School classes, both pray, both sing praises to GOD so, most people cannot tell the difference. They both act the same so that only GOD can actually know the difference. The tragic thing about this is that the *Heart* Christian will go to live eternally with GOD, and the *Mind* Christian will be told by GOD Himself *"Depart from me, you workers of iniquity, I never knew you."*

The *Heart* Christian is the one who, when they heard the Gospel told to them, came to realize that they were sinners and could not save themselves. So they turned to GOD for the *gift* of eternal life paid for by Jesus Christ who died on the Cross to pay for their sins. At that moment, Jesus came to live in their hearts, from then on. All past sins were forgiven and all future sins have a covering for the rest of their lives.

The *Mind* Christians heard the Gospel and realized they were sinners and set out to clean up their lives so GOD could save them. They never come to realize that only Jesus Christ and His death on the cross, and the shedding of His blood can wash the sinner clean and give them eternal life. They go through life trying to live a Holy life before GOD and man to *earn* eternal salvation. When

Jesus walked the Earth and taught His followers, He repeated over and over that no one can go to Heaven except through Him.

There are two groups of people, *both good people*, hoping for eternal live. One *knows* they have it, and the other *hopes* they have it. One group worships and works for GOD because they love Him and because it is just right. The other group worships GOD and works for Him hoping He will notice it and bless them and give them eternal life at the end of time. That is very sad.

BOTTOM LINE: Giving GOD control of our lives is the right thing to do.

Your Notes & Scriptures:

86 – THE TREE OF LIFE AND THE TREE OF DEATH

There is a Tree of Life and a Tree of Death. Both trees were planted in the Garden of Eden. GOD told Adam that he could eat from any tree in the garden except the Tree of Knowledge of Good and Evil, *the Tree of Death.* GOD told Adam and Eve that the day they ate from this tree, they would surely die.

Now, they died spiritually the day they rebelled against GOD and ate fruit from that tree. Also, they died physically in less than a thousand years, *one of GOD's days.* In fact, no one in that time lived to be one thousand years old. As a result of their rebellion, their sin against GOD, He drove them out of the Garden of Eden to keep them from eating from the Tree of Life and living forever in their fallen state.

So all mankind inherited a sinful nature from Adam. We have no way of changing that by our own power. Only the blood of Jesus Christ can wash a sinner clean and give eternal life. From then until the time that Jesus came, people could be saved by taking an animal of GOD's choice and shedding its blood to atone for their sin. That means that without the shedding of blood their sins were not covered.

About four thousand years later, Jesus Christ, GOD's Son, came down from Heaven and was born of a virgin girl. GOD Himself was His father and He destined Jesus to shed His blood for the final sacrifice for all mankind. After the death of Jesus Christ, no other sacrifice was needed for all eternity. What a grand thought that is; *AMEN*.

The spiritual leaders of that day had added so much to the law it was nothing like the original law given to Moses. Jesus had to spend over three years teaching the men He chose to be His apostles about the *real* law as it was written in Heaven.

The Tree of Knowledge of Good and Evil turned out to be the *Tree of Death*, because GOD pronounced death on Adam and Eve when they ate the forbidden fruit. That tree turned out to the *door* out of Paradise. The tree that Jesus was crucified on turned out to be the *Tree of Life*; the door back into Paradise, for all who will accept His sacrifice for their sins and turn their lives over to Him

BOTTOM LINE: We can only find out about these things in GOD's Word and probably will not know all of it until we go into GOD's presence and hear Him explain it.

Your Notes & Scriptures:

87 – CHRISTIAN WORKS

In the King James Version of the Bible, in the book of 1ˢᵗ Corinthians, Chapter 3, verses 11 through 15, we read these words. *"For other foundation can no man lay than that is laid which is Jesus Christ. Now if any man build on this foundation, gold, silver, precious stones, wood, hay, stubble; every man's work shall be made manifest: for the day shall declare it, because it will be revealed by fire; and the fire shall try every man's work of what sort it is. If any man's work abide, which he has built thereupon, he shall receive a reward. If any man's work shall be burned, he shall suffer loss: although he shall be saved; yet so as by fire."*

We know that gold, silver, and precious stones can go through a fire and not be totally destroyed. So what did GOD mean when He named these three items? Could it mean to love GOD with all our hearts, soul, and minds? Could it mean for Christians to love one another and try to help each other, our neighbors, and anyone else who needs it? Could it be to let our lights shine before the world so people could see GOD showing Himself through us? Could it mean that we should go to church prayed up and ready to receive GOD's message He has for us on that day? To sum it up, I think it means all of the above and much, much more. We don't need to be *playing* Christian. We need to get serious about it.

What did GOD mean when He said *wood, hay, and stubble*? He knows that all three of these things will burn up very fast in a fire. Could this be the religious folks who want to go to Heaven, but think that they have to be *good* and work hard in the church, and keep themselves clean at all times? Are they the ones who think that if their *good deeds* outweigh the *bad deeds*, they will make into Heaven?

Let's talk about this a little bit. We know that Jesus, GOD's Son, had to give His own life to pay for my sins because, even if I tried to die for my own sins, that would not be enough. I don't have anything more precious than my own life, and if that would not pay the debt for my sins, what else do I have to give? GOD has already said that my own works are nothing but filthy rags in His sight. It took me many years to learn one simple thing; GOD does not want my works, of *wood, hay, and stubble.* He wants to do His work through me. In other words, He just wants me to report for duty each day.

BOTTOM LINE: None of us would adopt a little child and then let it starve. Neither will our GOD. AMEN!

Your Notes & Scriptures:

88 – TRUE BELIEF

"For God so loved the world that he gave his only begotten Son that whosoever believes in him should not perish but have everlasting life." John 3:16

Almost anyone who is asked if they believe in Jesus Christ will say yes. The problem is that there is more to believing in Jesus Christ than just saying it. When the Gospel is brought to a person they must first listen. Then the Holy Spirit will convince them that they are a sinner and must make a complete turn-around, forsake their sins and surrender to Jesus for a cleansing of past sins. After that a training time begins. God has a place of service for everyone who will turn to Him.

Don't think that GOD is a giant task-master. GOD is so tender and forgiving with more love than we can imagine. You will not know that until you try it. GOD seems to want us to try Him and see if He will keep all His promises. The ones who do try Him will find a fulfilled life that lost people can only imagine. While GOD is not going to condone our sin, He will help us out of our mistakes with loving care. We just can't have it any better than that.

I heard a story about a soldier who was fatally wounded on the battle field. He called for his leader and told him that he was about to go out in eternity and he did not know GOD in any way. The leader remembered when he was a child, his mother taught him the Bible verse John 3:16, written above. When the leader quoted that Bible verse to him, the soldier believed it and came to Jesus for salvation before he died. That's the way GOD is, in that He will bend very low to save the soul of a human being. The soul inside of every person is very precious to GOD. He will seek and save anyone who will listen and ask Him for the gift of salvation.

When we come to GOD for forgiveness of sin and salvation, it makes us strangers on this Earth. We, like Jesus, become the enemy of Satan, and he will do everything in his power to keep us from serving GOD like GOD wants us to. That is some of the trouble we will face as long as we live on this Earth.

BOTTOM LINE: No matter what we have to face, our retirement plan is out of this world.

Your Notes & Scriptures:

89 – RIGHTEOUS

Can Christians be holy enough or righteous enough to appear in GOD's presence? *NO*, because we are of the Earth which was cursed when mankind disobeyed GOD in the Garden of Eden. We have been born with the sinful bloodline of Adam.

When GOD made the plan of salvation, He knew that only He could supply the holiness to enter Heaven. He made the plan to redeem mankind by coming to Earth in the likeness of mankind, but without the sinful blood of humans. This all means that all we have or ever hope to have comes from GOD Himself. GOD had demonstrated His loving care and concern for His creation by giving us His own righteous so we could stand in His presence after this life.

GOD has given us the Bible for a guide while we live on this Earth. Any kind of situation is covered in the Bible and GOD invites us to come before Him, through the Holy Spirit, and make our requests known. I don't see how we could wish for more than that.

What advantage is it to live in GOD's Will? When Christians decide to surrender all to GOD they find love, joy, peace, and a great crowd of Christian brothers and sisters to enjoy and have fellowship with. One thing we should be aware of is that the Devil hates it when Christians enjoy fellowship with other Christians, and enjoy the presence of GOD when we talk to Him. Satan will do everything in his power to disrupt Christian joy and testimony. He will throw every temptation he can in our paths. We must remember that Jesus said, *"When people hate you, remember they hated me first."*

There is an age old problem with humankind today which could be worse than we think. So many people believe that if they do good deeds and live right, they will make it into Heaven. That is a tragic mistake that is going to destroy many, many people. The hardest thing to convince people of is that they are sinners and have a need for a Savior. Many will say, I am alright or I am better than most Christians.

BOTTOM LINE: Praise GOD, and be thankful for what we have.

Your Notes & Scriptures:

90 – WHO DOES GOD CALL?

Who does GOD call to Jesus Christ for forgiveness of sin and eternal salvation?

The records that I know about suggest that He calls those who need it; like everyone, including the lowly and needy and those who cannot help themselves. Jesus first called twelve men who were common working men. They were uneducated but willing to follow Him while He was teaching them the plan for the final stage of time as we know it.

The nation of Israel had all the records of GOD's plan from the beginning. But they had added so much to GOD's Word that Jesus had to start from the beginning and teach the Apostles the whole truth about His plan for the final end of the Earth. The whole point is, Jesus did not come after the righteous people, he came after sinners who would repent and turn to Him for forgiveness of sin and eternal salvation.

GOD knew that when He forgave people of their sins, they would still live in the sinful flesh and would slip and sin sometimes, so He made a provision for forgiveness of sin for the rest of the person's life. Don't be foolish enough to think GOD will let us romp through this world enjoying sin daily after we receive His eternal salvation. Saved of not, sin has a price, which is always bad stuff.

For example, if we go out and turn away from GOD and lose a limb or something else, GOD will forgive us for the sin, but He will not make us a new limb. We will have to live the rest of our lives without it.

Jesus never spoke a single word that is not true and useful to us for instruction and a guide through this life. We know that the Devil will try everything in his power to stop us from studying our Bibles, because that is the *food* that feeds our souls and causes us to grow in grace. In studying the Bible, we learn more about Jesus and all His teachings while He was on this Earth. That is very important because GOD wants us to become as much like Jesus as possible. Although we face many distractions daily, it really is possible to grow to be *almost* like Jesus.

I wish I could say, "Watch me for your example," but if you did, you would be in bad shape. I find out every day just how clever the old Devil is and how he fools me all the time. I thank GOD daily for His power to help me overcome the temptations that come all the time.

BOTTOM LINE: We *must* trust GOD with our problems.

Your Notes & Scriptures:

91 – SOME EXPLINATION

There is a certain passage in the Bible that may need further explanation. It is found in the New Testament Book of 1st Corinthians, Chapter thirteen, verses 8-10, and 13.

*"Love never ends. As for prophecies, they will pass away; as for tongues, they will cease; as for knowledge it will pass away, for we know in part and we prophesy in part. But when the **perfect** comes, the partial will pass away. And now faith, hope, and love abide, these three: but the greatest of these is love."*

What is the **perfect** mentioned above? The *perfect* is the printed Word of GOD, the Bible. Some of the *signs* were given to the early Church to prove that a person had accepted Jesus as their personal Savior. The leaders did not have any other way of knowing who was a true Christian and who was not. Since the Bible has been printed and is now available to everyone, these signs are not necessary. Today, people are witnessed to about the salvation written in the Bible. If people will not believe the words written in the Bible, neither will they believe signs if GOD should give them.

The greatest of the three remaining signs of Faith, Hope, and Love, is *Love*. There are several reasons for that. The greatest of all is the fact that GOD loved mankind even when He could not find one righteous man on the Earth. Jesus said in one place that He came to seek and save that which was lost. We know the He was talking about the soul of man. Every living person has a soul and that is what GOD wants to redeem for Himself. GOD breathed into

Adam's nostrils and gave him a living soul above all other living creatures. The soul of man is very precious to GOD and He will keep trying to draw people to Himself until time has ended.

GOD also gives His love to the ones who will trust Him for forgiveness of sin and eternal salvation. GOD gives His children the ability to love others as He does. The Love given at the point of salvation must grow as that person grows in the knowledge and likeness of Jesus Christ. It is amazing how one can grow in grace and love people who are unlovable. It is amazing how we can actually learn to love like GOD does.

BOTTOM LINE: GOD's free gift of salvation is available to every person on this Earth. They just need to hear about it.

Your Notes & Scriptures:

92 – DOERS OF THE WORD

It is written in the Bible Book of James, that Christians should be *doers of GOD's Word and not hearers only*. When we are hearers only, we deceive ourselves into thinking that GOD needs us. Actually, a Christian who does nothing will receive nothing from the Lord. GOD cannot bless our steps if we don't ever take one. We become like a big old fat kid that sits in the parents lap for hours and hours. That makes my legs get numb just thinking about it. Christians, who are idle all the time spiritually, are no good to GOD or Man.

The condition of our world and our government seems to point toward the end time of the world as we know it. How tragic would it be if our sons and daughters were lost and could not go into eternity with GOD? It seems that the loved ones closest to us are sometimes overlooked.

It seems that in the times we live in, with all the distractions we face every day, it makes it harder to remain true to GOD and our church activities. If we don't support the work that the church does, we will not support anything else except our own selves. It seems to me that the more we become involved in the workings of our church, the deeper we will go into our personal lives with regard to our neighbors, friends, and relatives.

Jesus was not making idle talk when He said, "*..let your light shine before the world,*" because when people see that, they will take notice of it and some will want what we have. The thing that we should be concerned about is that our spiritual lights are bright enough for the world to see.

We should get our spiritual bath, *or cleaning*, when we attend church on a regular basis. It we get into the habit of going regularly, we will soon get to where we miss it when we miss a Sunday. No matter how mature we may get in our spiritual lives we still need to be cleaned up. Only GOD can do that. If we had that power, we wouldn't need GOD. The more we learn about GOD's holiness, the more we see that, apart from GOD, we have no holiness at all.

BOTTOM LINE: If we are close to the end times, it makes good sense to be a little more attentive to things that GOD has given us to do.

Your Notes & Scriptures:

93 – STRANGE THINGS ARE HAPPENING

Strange and terrible things are happening around the world. Many people are being killed and many are starving and homeless. It seems that the words of Jesus are coming closer and closer. *"When you see these things coming, look up for your redemption draws near."* Some people will say, *this* must happen or *that* must happen, but I have heard several learned people say, all things that must come to pass has already come to pass.

I do not have the knowledge or skill to dispute that, but within my limited understanding, I have to agree with the latter, that Jesus can come this minute or whenever GOD sends Him to get His children. I personally believe that what we are seeing is the beginning of sorrows that Jesus spoke about when He was asked about the end time. The moral decline and the great damage of property in our own country seem to agree with the words Jesus spoke about the end time.

One good thing about today is that the number of churches, although declining, is still in the hundreds of thousands. It looks like the Gospel of Jesus Christ is *alive* and well. There are over five thousand missionaries from one single denomination, and there are several denominations that are preaching the pure Gospel. Although some of the missionaries are being hindered or killed, they are doing a great job and leading many to know Jesus Christ. But, in our country, we may have to become bolder in witnessing to our love ones, friends, and neighbors. Just how far we are willing to go will depend on how much we care about them.

Personally I have discovered that my own affairs, take a lot of my time. I think that I have my *things* to look after and enjoy, and that I don't have much time for outside activities. After discovering that, I have to decide just how much I am willing to serve GOD, and how much I want to serve myself. When I serve myself, I am serving an old body that is headed to the grave. But when I serve GOD I am preparing for eternity with the perfect GOD in the perfect Paradise.

The time a Christian spends on this Earth is only a time of training for eternity. Our Manual, the Bible, is complete and true in every detail. There is no event or problem we face that is not covered in our Bibles. One big problem we face continually is that the roaring lion, *the Devil,* will do anything to keep us from reading and studying our Bibles. But, GOD does give us the power and strength to overcome all the trials the Devil throws our way.

BOTTOM LINE: We should just report for duty and let GOD do the protecting *thing*.

Your Notes & Scriptures:

94 – PILLS, PILLS

How many *pills* does it take to stay alive these days? I am beginning to check my ears often to see if pills are coming out of them. I have pills to sleep and pills to wake me up. I have happy pills and pills to keep everything in check. I have pills for all my ills. I have a handful in the morning that keeps me alive until night and another handful at night to last me until morning. Having said all that, I wonder what GOD thinks about all this medicine we have invented for our health.

I am reminded of what GOD said through Paul in one of his letters to the churches. He wrote that Christians' bodies are the temple of the Holy Spirit and if any one destroys GOD's temple, GOD will destroy them. I personally think that has permitted all the new medicines to be discovered for people to use in a responsible way.

We all know that GOD is the great healer and does heal people according to His plan. We must remember that GOD is not going to pet and pamper these old bodies of ours. When we have a need for medicine or a doctor's care, it is our responsibility to go and get the help we need. Today there are many Christian doctors available to help us. I am convinced that GOD Himself provides the doctors for us as we need them. The Apostle Luke was a doctor and traveled with the Apostle Paul on many of his journeys. If the practice of medicine dates back that far, we should use it the same way Paul did and thank GOD for providing it.

GOD heals people according to His Will and purpose. I am sure that most people remember the time when Jesus went to the pool where the angel troubled the water sometimes and whoever stepped into the water first was healed of all sickness. When Jesus came to the pool, He saw one man that had been crippled a long time so He healed the man and left. Now, Jesus could have waved His hand and healed everyone there, but Jesus had a higher purpose for healing just one man. That healing was done on the Sabbath and once again caused the Jews to condemn Jesus for healing on the Sabbath because they said that no work could be done on the Sabbath. That was another reason they crucified Jesus.

BOTTOM LINE: When it comes time, go ahead and take those pills.

Your Notes & Scriptures:

95 – A DISCUSSION

THIS IS A DISCUSSION ABOUT THE GREAT WHITE THRONE JUDGEMENT. This is the final Judgment of all humankind.

The Bible says that the *dead* will be judged at this time. After this, the new Heaven and Earth will be put into place. At this final Judgment, all bodies of the lost will be brought back from wherever they are and reunited with the people. Those are the bodies that are in the depths of the sea, the ones that were cremated, the ones that were torn into little pieces, and the ones in the graves. Then, all those who did not receive salvation by faith in Jesus Christ will stand before GOD's Throne for judgment of their works.

The Bible says that at this judgment the books will be opened and another book will be opened. Some people believe that the *books* meant the books of the Bible, and the *other* refers to the Book of Life. We need to remember that the Rapture of the Church will have already taken place and the Saints will be judged before the Judgment Seat of Christ, from the Lamb's Book of Life. At this point the tribulation period, *seven years*, and then the thousand year millennium rein have already passed.

Here are some thoughts about the Book of Life mentioned at this last judgment. I believe that when GOD, or the trinity of GOD, made the plan for the creation and the Earth to be filled with people, He recorded every name of every person that would be born on this Earth from start to finish. When a person's death without GOD comes to pass, their name is blotted out from the Book of Life mentioned here. The Bible says that if the person's name is not found in the Book of Life, he is cast into the lake of fire.

Jesus made mention of the fact that if a person would come to Him by faith and accept His free gift of forgiveness of sin and eternal life, He would not blot their name from the Book of Life. Some have said that this is where Christians can lose their salvation because Jesus could not blot their name out of the book if their name was not in there to start with. What people don't realize is that Jesus is talking about two different books. The Book of Life covers all the people born on this Earth. The Lamb's Book of Life covers the Christians, the Saints of the Church.

BOTTOM LINE: Wouldn't it be horrible to be saved and serve GOD for a long time and then slip and commit one small sin and have our name blotted out of His book? Well, it's not going to happen!

Your Notes & Scriptures:

96 – GOD WITH US

Christians: Is GOD really with us 24/7 when we surrender to His guiding Spirit?

One way we can know that GOD is with us is, when we start the day with GOD, all the decisions we make during the day seems to be easier and more satisfying. If we stop and think, we make many decisions during each day. It's like GOD is the Father and we are the children, ever learning as we go along in this world. I personally think GOD enjoys our company more than we enjoy His, unless we are truly surrendered to His leadership throughout the day. What a great feeling it is to be in the presence of GOD.

When we go to church, GOD is always there too, to receive our prayers and cleanse us from all unrighteousness. In fact, the reason we go to church is to worship GOD and receive our Spiritual bath, and be restored to full fellowship with GOD. If we let ourselves get filled up with the *world*, it is hard to get the full benefit from our church experience. Trying to serve GOD outside the church is a complete waste of time and effort. If we say that we can serve GOD just as good on the golf course or at the fishing hole we are fooling ourselves and are far away from actually following GOD. The church is actually our *headquarters* where we receive our instructions from GOD and His Word. If we try to make it anything else, we destroy its purpose completely.

The Bible says, *"How good and how pleasant for brothers to dwell together in unity."* What strength we gain from each other when we can agree on everything.

Even when we don't agree with each other, we still find strength when we meet together. That is a reminder that we should not neglect the assembling of ourselves together when the time comes.

I am sure that most Christians have experienced GOD's help in our physical world on the little things that we get into. I have had GOD to help me out of a *spiritual ditch* when I was alone and could not get out by myself. GOD has helped me with my kids when I didn't have the answer. GOD has given me words to say when I did not have any. GOD has closed my mouth when I was about to say the wrong thing. The list goes on and on. Believe it or not, GOD *can* be trusted.

BOTTOM LINE: Try as we may, we cannot live a Christian life without a close relationship with GOD.

Your Notes & Scriptures:

97 – THE CORD OF SIN

Who can break the cord of sin from a person's life? Can a person really live *good enough* to earn eternal life in Heaven? In my personal opinion, that cord is made of the toughest steel and no person is able to break it by themselves. We know that if GOD is willing to save a person and take them to live with Him in Heaven, then He would surely be willing to break that cord Himself.

It seems that very often, after a person is saved, they slide back into sin and GOD has to come and rescue them once again. The Devil does not miss a chance to entice a Christian to sin and break fellowship with GOD. That is why a Christian must be on guard 24/7.

I believe GOD wants people who really want Him to save their souls and be their guide while they live on this Earth. It is the greatest thing to really seek after GOD. GOD said in His Word that, *"He who seeks after GOD will find Him"*. Finding GOD is the most joyful and humbling experience any person can have. Instead of that joy bringing laughter and gala feelings, it usually brings tears of joy. I don't think that anyone could really explain it but anyone who will trust Jesus Christ who paid for their sins, will surely have that experience which will never be forgotten.

The Apostle Peter was arrested and put into prison with chains on both arms and attached to two soldiers. One angel came in the night and caused the chains to fall off and set Peter free. Then all the prison doors opened all by themselves and Peter just walked out of the prison. None of the other prisoners or the guards woke up until the next morning. Since GOD has a Host of Angels, and just one could do that, I don't think He would have any trouble protecting us while we live on this Earth.

We are like soldiers caught behind enemy lines. We must be alert and do the work of GOD while we have the opportunity. We also must realize that each time we start to do any of GOD's work we will face opposition from the enemy, Satan. The Devil hates it when we do anything for GOD, or when we read our Bibles, or when we pray for someone else or even ourselves, or even when we go to Church and worship and enjoy fellowship with our Christian brothers and sisters.

BOTTOM LINE: I believe if we would ponder the thoughts and seek after GOD and the knowledge of GOD, we would surely live more peaceful lives and be fruitful.

Your Notes & Scriptures:

98 – TEMPTED TO SIN

TEMPTATION: Why are Christians tempted to sin and turn against GOD? We all know what sin is because the Holy Spirit, who lives in our souls, reminds us when we are about to give in to temptation and sin against our Lord and Savior Jesus Christ. I believe the Bible makes it very clear that the Devil is at war against GOD and all of His children. Any time a Christian starts to do something for GOD or even something good, they will find opposition from the evil spirit world. There is no way that we can get away from that, however, one of the greatest promises from GOD is that He will not allow any temptation to come upon us that we are not able to resist.

That means we don't *have* to sin. If GOD is willing to give us the power to resist, we should be willing to use it. So, here's the *BIG QUESTION*; why do we sin? It seems that when GOD said that the *"Spirit is willing, but the flesh is weak,"* that applies to all of us. I believe the reason GOD said that is, He knows we still live in a sinful world and we fight a never ending battle with the forces of evil.

GOD also knows that we will not always resist the temptation to sin. For that reason GOD has promised us forgiveness for life so that we would not be saved one day and lose it the next. It seems to me that this promise from GOD Himself should be enough for us to praise and glorify Him for the rest of our lives. I think we should at least praise GOD as much as we do sports teams, like my favorites, the Cowboys or Rangers when they win. If we stop and think about it, GOD wins all the time. He never loses. Jesus said that He would not lose anyone who comes to Him for forgiveness of sin and eternal salvation. So let us learn how to praise and glorify GOD daily.

There is another area of temptation we face often; to *overdo* when GOD gives a chore or a job to do. Sometimes when that happens, we tend to run out in front of GOD and start doing things our way. We hear many testimonies of Christians in GOD's service who have done that and failed in some way. They then have to back up and call on GOD to clean up the mess. GOD is so gentle with His children that it is easy to love Him and desire to do His will.

BOTTOM LINE: We need to test GOD and see if He will give us a fresh start after we have failed Him in some way. I know he will, from experience.

Your Notes & Scriptures:

99 – BE A MAN

We often hear the phrase; *"Be a man"*. What does that mean exactly? In some foreign countries the women walk a few steps behind their husbands. Here in America, the men often walk a step or two behind their wives. It seems that somewhere between there and here things have changed.

In some other countries, the men rule over the house and family and are responsible for their welfare and safety. Here in America, when some ask a man about his homestead, he will often say, *"Ask my wife."* I will tell you for certain that things have changed somewhere along the trail of advancement of humankind. I am not complaining; my little ole wife is smart enough to handle all of that. I think the real problem here is, when someone is willing to make decisions for us, we are willing to let them. Maybe we should be more willing to step up and handle things like *real men*. This thinking begs one question; what is a *real man* in GOD'S eyes?

Noah trusted GOD enough to build a large ark on dry ground with no water in sight. David trusted GOD enough to face and kill a giant twice his size, without any hesitation or fear. *David picked up five stones. He did not think that he might miss the first time but he knew the giant had four brothers and he had to be ready for them too.*

At the end of Job's trouble, GOD said to him, *"stand up like a man and I will speak to you."* At the beginning of the Church, when the Holy Spirit came on those 120 members, they stood and preached Jesus Christ boldly even when some were beaten and some were killed.

It seems that GOD defines a *man* as one who will stand up by faith in the face of danger and proclaim the Gospel whenever the opportunity comes. So far, few of us have faced any real danger while witnessing for Jesus Christ. The day may come however when our faith will be challenged in our own country or town.

We tend to think a real man must be big and strong and fearless. Somehow I do not think that GOD thinks that way. Some of GOD's greatest servants are meek and lowly at heart and have a certain radiance about them that only comes from knowing GOD.

GOD is the only one who can take an old beat up worn out person who has wasted their life in sin, and make them into a beautiful person, clean and holy.

BOTTOM LINE: I will probably never reach the *manhood* that I should, but I am going to try.

Your Notes & Scriptures:

100 – THE LAW FULFILLED

Jesus Christ came to Earth to pay the sin debt for all mankind. When that was done, He returned to Heaven. WHAT DID HE LEAVE BEHIND WHEN HE LEFT?

He left an example of a lifestyle that was unknown before He came. He fulfilled the law and raised it to a higher level. He said no more *an eye for an eye* or *a tooth for a tooth.* He said if someone slaps you on one cheek, turn the other. He said, if someone sues you by the law, settle it before you get to court. He said to take the *wrong* if you have to. In other words, He said to live peaceable with all men if possible. He also said obey the laws of the land. I believe Jesus meant that it would be hard to find fault with someone who obeys the law and lives at peace with all people around him.

After Jesus departed Earth, He sent His Spirit to indwell His *saved* believers. The spirit gave Christians the power to keep the words of Jesus and endure the persecution that would come because of the Gospel. He did not leave His disciples helpless, but He gave each one power to carry out the assignment for them. Jesus did not demand service from His disciples that they could not do. The service to GOD through Jesus Christ is to use what each one of us has, and use it where we are. GOD Himself does the calling to special service such as Ministers of the Gospel or workers in the Church.

Jesus Christ left behind His Word which was later written down and bound into a book called the Bible. His Word in so clear that no one has an excuse to sin after having been saved. However, Jesus knew that we are all frail humans and we will sin from time to time. So He made a way to forgive sins after salvation by giving us access to GOD through His name and He will intercede for us before GOD. That may sound a little confusing, but we should have the faith that GOD will keep His promises to us.

Jesus formed and left behind His *Church* and leaders to build upon His Word through the power of the Holy Spirit, *the overseer of the Church*. What this means is that all activities of the Church are under the direct control of GOD the Holy Spirit, who is guiding to our Church leaders.

BOTTOM LINE: I thank GOD for the men and women who serve and are led by the Spirit.

Your Notes & Scriptures:

ABOUT THE AUTHOR

Willie Holt was the Number Two child in a farming family consisting of his Mother and Father and ten kids. He spent most of his young years as a farmer before entering a two year career in the Air Force as a secret code specialist in the Airways and Air Communications Service, headquartered in Alaska. Following military service Willie spent time working in the Texas oil fields before starting a carpentry building business. For the last half of his working career he was an aircraft inspector at LTV Aircraft Corporation in Arlington Texas, working on many major government projects.

Willie lost his first wife, Bobbie, to illness in the year he retired. A year later he married Mary. Willie and Mary have traveled to Israel, taken seven cruises to much of the world, and settled in Forney Texas where he writes a Weekly Column for the local newspaper. He is also active in the First Baptist Church of Forney. Willie's interests now are playing golf, playing gospel music, playing dominos, and of course, writing.

Made in the USA
Charleston, SC
14 November 2015